The Wonderful
World
of Yogurt

THE WONDERFUL WORLD OF YOGURT

by DOROTHY PARKER

A Martin Dale Book

HAWTHORN BOOKS, INC.
PUBLISHERS / *New York*

The author is indebted to the Integral Yoga Institute, 227 West 13th Street, New York, New York, for the following recipes: Still Another Fruit Soup (page 30), Carrot-Cauliflower Casserole (page 78), Sprout Salad (page 79), and Carrot-Raisin Salad (page 80).

For my parents,
Edith Ives Parker
and
Robert Emerson Parker

FOREWORD:

WHAT IS YOGURT?

It is astonishing to me that there are people in the
United States still unacquainted with the miracle food
yogurt, timid souls who have never tasted it, under-
privileged folk who have never even heard of it! Let
this unhappy day pass forthwith. Every child should
know its wonders, every grown-up should reap its
benefits, every cook should appreciate its versatility.

Whether bought at the market or prepared at home,
yogurt is a dairy product made from milk to which
yogurt culture has been added. The milk is left in a

warm situation for a number of hours until it has acquired a soft, custardlike texture and a clean, rather tart taste. The flavor is unique—quite unlike that of anything else in the food world. It has been likened to pineapple, but that seems to me to miss it. Some tasters cannot distinguish it from that of buttermilk, which is made from skim milk and is lower in calories than yogurt. Sour cream may come closer, though yogurt is more tart. Sour cream, being made from sweet cream, is much higher than yogurt in fat and carbohydrates. An 8-ounce glass of whole milk has about 150–170 calories; an equal quantity of plain yogurt has only 100 or so. Yogurt and sour cream mixed half and half provides a taste experience much favored by some Russian-Americans and a compromise in the calorie-counting area.

As commercially prepared in this country, yogurt is made from homogenized, pasteurized cows' milk with half the butterfat removed and proteins and vitamins added. (In Bulgaria the usual starter is a combination of goats' and water buffaloes' milk, which is twice as rich in butterfat to begin with as cows' milk.) The company that introduced yogurt commercially in this country nearly went broke on it until they remembered the sweet tooth of the average American and added preserved fruits to the plain yogurt—strawberries first, closely followed by raspberries, apricots, blueberries, cherries, pineapple, and so on. Now Americans eat well over 100,000,000 cups of commercial yogurt a year, most of this on the East and West coasts. Perhaps the great heartland of America is making its own yogurt at home, thus complicating this interesting statistic.

Yogurt is easy to make, as I will presently explain (see Chapter 2, "Method and Mystique"). And it is a nearly perfect food, better for you than milk, being lower in cholesterol and calories, higher in nutrients and natural medicinal benefits (see Chapter 1, "History and Health").

Little Miss Muffet, for all we know, may have been eating yogurt when that terrifying arachnid came along. "Curds and whey" are what result when milk is allowed to sour or ferment through the action of bacteria from the air which settle in it; curds are the solids that form, whey the liquid (mostly water) remainder. To get true yogurt you must introduce a specific yogurt culture into the milk, not just any old germs flying around in the atmosphere. I doubt if Miss Muffet ate yogurt: Neither the British nor the French, whom we can thank for Mother Goose, have ever been strong on yogurt.

One yogurt-resisting friend of mine said she just didn't like the idea of "all those bacteria inside of me." But of course, her body is loaded with bacteria at all times—it couldn't function without them—and friendly little *Baccillus bulgaricus* (the yogurt microbe) is no more a germ in the pejorative sense than is yeast, without which no risen crumb of bread would pass her lips. He is, in fact, a good deal better than harmless, being an active, positive aid to life and health.

Another nonfancier who said, "I just can't stand yogurt," when questioned closely about how and when and under what circumstances he had tried it, admitted that he had never in his life eaten it and that it was the *sound of the word* he didn't like. It's true that its hard, abrupt, rather choking sound is not mellifluous. If that is your stumbling block, perhaps you should choose one of yogurt's other names so that you might no longer miss this smooth, rare treat. It is called many things in many lands: for example, *yaghourt, madzoon* or *matsoon, koumiss kefir, prostokvasha, kisele mleko, leban* or *liban*. If these don't seem to roll off your tongue like nectar of the gods, make up your own word. Call yogurt whatever you like, as long as you try it. Try it in all its fine, elegant, snowy purity—and then move on among the 200-odd recipes in this book.

D. P.

CONTENTS

xi

*The Wonderful
World
of Yogurt*

Chapter 1

HISTORY
AND
HEALTH

The story of yogurt, that wondrous new-old food, stretches back into history nearly as far as man himself. Anyway, it is surely as old as man and beast as a symbiotic work team; as soon as herding became part of the nomadic life that foreran for centuries the domestication of animals, there was doubtless yogurt. The Old Testament has Abraham waxing strong on goats'-milk yogurt (and it was probably responsible for Sarah's long reproductive cycle). Solomon's wisdom is surely somewhere attributed to his consumption of yogurt, and ask the Bulgarians about Methuselah's age!

Earlier than the third century, Persians were making yogurt from the milk of goats, sheep, camels, and water buffaloes (they are also credited by some historians with inventing cheese). Genghis Khan, it is recorded, devoured yogurt by the crockful, fed it to his armies, and used it to preserve meat; his preferred starter was a combination of mares' and yaks' milk. For millennia Mongolians, Arabs, and other Middle Eastern peoples have been souring the milk of various milk-producing mammals into yogurt, and for millennia the people of these regions have been notable for life spans far beyond the world average. There is evidence to support the notion that the Mongol hordes poured fresh milk into their saddle bags and let the heat of their steeds' bodies work the milk into yogurt as they tore around, ravishing the Middle European countryside. A pretty picture!

Yogurt has *always* been a staple of the diet in many parts of the world. Today in the West it is Bulgaria that is chiefly associated with yogurt, and for very good reason: It has long been one of that country's principal foods and is considered responsible for the people's unusual record of health and longevity. Bulgarians, as a group, apparently remain vigorous and virile into advanced age; compared with Americans, the difference is frightening. About 180 times as many Bulgars as Americans survive past the century mark!

Bulgarians don't become bald, their hair does not turn gray, and many continue to beget offspring at amazing ages. All this they usually attribute to their consumption of yogurt, which for some individuals goes as high as six pounds a day.

The Bulgarians claim too that only in the highlands of their country can be found the proper microbe for the fermenting of milk into yogurt, and that yogurt made anywhere else in the world does not deserve the name. The name of the culture that does in fact make yogurt everywhere else in the world is *Bacillus bulgaricus*, sometimes by itself, sometimes in combination with *Bacillus lacticum*. These 2 truly remarkable organisms preserved their mystery until around 1900, when they were isolated by Dr. Elie Metchnikoff, the Russian bacteriologist who then headed the Pasteur Institute in Paris and who was the winner of a Nobel Prize in 1908. Yogurt did not cross the Atlantic to any extent, however, until 1920, when it was imported by the Rosell Bacteriological Dairy Institute of the La Trappe Monastery in Canada. (The yogurt culture that I use and recommend is packaged by the Rosell Institute.) Since that time much research has been done on yogurt's nature and properties, and it emerges as one of nature's most perfect foods and one of modern medicine's most valuable aids.

The list of diseases and disorders that yogurt has been credited with curing is formidable. Here, in part, it is:

abdominal stress of
  pregnancy
arteriosclerosis
arthritis
autointoxication
cholera
colitis
constipation
diarrhea

dysentery
flatulence
gallstones
halitosis
hepatitis
kidney disorders
migraine
skin disease (and allergies)
typhoid fever

Yogurt is a busy and versatile aid to digestion. It controls the action of the intestine in stimulating the kidneys favorably; it breaks down casein, dissolves calcium, and contains, manufactures, and renders accessible the whole group of B vitamins so important to health and long life. It has a higher percentage of vitamins A and D than does the milk from which it was made, and it is higher in protein and lower in fat than that same milk.

Whole milk takes 3 hours to digest; yogurt digests in 1. Thus it satisfies the appetite better than milk. The beneficial bacteria in yogurt make it a natural antibiotic; its natural enemies are the harmful bacteria of the large intestine. It can also counteract the hateful effects some people experience from the use of manufactured antibiotics. Yogurt acts as an arrester of putrefaction, thereby ameliorating the process of aging and all kinds of unpleasant disorders often associated with advancing years. As a dietary supplement and regulator it has often been recommended in pediatric and geriatric practices.

Since the yogurt bacillus is not a usual inhabitant of the intestinal tract and does not just set up shop and keep reproducing itself there, it must be eaten regularly for a person to derive the optimum benefit from it. Fortunately, it is a case of "all this and heaven too," for the formulas in this book not only keep you healthy but at the same time also produce libations and feasts that are sheer ambrosia. Get into the yogurt habit for both enjoyment and health.

Chapter 2

METHOD
AND
MYSTIQUE

As with the baking of bread, there is a mystique surrounding the making of yogurt that is pure nonsense. Like the much maligned soufflé, unreasonably feared by neophyte cooks, yogurt is easy as pie to make and to make well—consistently, with no trouble or fuss. I have never had a "failure" and am sure I never shall. The only trick, as in bread-making, is maintaining a more-or-less steady temperature over a period of some hours. And that can be accomplished with great ease by anyone who has an oven, a double boiler, a source of warm water, or a blanket.

You can start with any kind of milk (see Chapter 1, "History and Health," for other animal sources—but that's not what I mean, cows' milk being the one usually available in this country). Pasteurized whole milk, homogenized or not, in cartons or bottles, from the store or your milkman, is fine. So is powdered milk that you have shaken up with water, or condensed or evaporated milk (which come in those little cans that are so hard to flatten for recycling). Or a combination of these. My own favorite is 1 part evaporated milk to 3 parts milk made from powdered skim milk and tap water. The only thing *not* to start with is raw, unpasteurized milk. Or rather, if you do start with milk right from the cow, boil it first for 10 or 15 minutes to kill the competing bacteria that may be in it and then cool it to lukewarm.

To your milk add the yogurt culture that you have bought at the market or health-food store. Use at least 1 teaspoon to a quart. (Culture is still expensive—over $2 for a ⅛-ounce packet. But think of how far it had to travel—all the way from Bulgaria.) If you can't find any yogurt culture where you market, you will undoubtedly be able to find a container of commercial yogurt at the store's dairy counter. Use that, 3 tablespoons to 1 quart of milk.

Stir or blend your mixture a bit and pour it into some kind of glass or ceramic containers with covers (I use 1-quart Mason jars); *don't* fill the jars to the top. Then put them into a warm-water bath and let them sit in it for a few hours. I usually pop the jars into warm water in a large stew pot and put the pot in the just-barely-turned-on oven, set to the cool side of the "warm" marking. Some yogurt-makers with pilot-light gas ovens leave their jars in the turned-off oven; the pilot light provides enough warmth. If your oven is too flighty to keep a low, even heat (it should stay between 90° and 115° F.) for a few hours, then perhaps your kitchen sink will do: Surround your jars with warm water, which you can change from time to time as it cools. Or put the milk and culture into the top of a double boiler, over water that you keep hot, not boiling. If these ideas don't appeal to you, then put your milk and culture into a casserole, cover it, wrap the dish in a warm woolen blanket or a bunch of sweaters, and leave it somewhere overnight.

The only trouble with leaving the yogurt overnight is that you may be asleep, and really, ideally, at least the first time you try it, you ought to be able to check the progress of your yogurt from time to time by sticking your finger in it and tasting and feeling it. The number of hours the process takes varies with the amount of culture you've put in, the temperature that's maintained, and weather conditions. When the yogurt has developed that good, smart taste and its consistency is like rennet custard, then whisk it out of the warmth and into the coolth: refrigerate it. It may take 3 hours or 5 or 7 to reach the proper consistency, depending. If you leave it in the warmth too long, then you may get a cheesy texture you won't care for. And the longer it sits, the tarter it gets.

Some people add to their milk a packet of plain

gelatin, softened in cool tap water first. (I don't because I prefer the texture I get without it.) That can be useful if you want a thicker, more jellylike product. (Be sure to mix in the gelatin very well when you add it, or you'll get thin yogurt with a leather top on it.) If you want your yogurt more liquid, add water to your milk to begin with or add water afterward, simply stirring it in or whirring it with the yogurt in a blender.

Now that yogurt has become in some circles a chic, fashionable "in" food, there are even machines manufactured and sold for the specific purpose of yogurt-making. They are simply groups of covered square glass containers that fit snugly onto an electric hot tray that maintains a low heat. I'm sure they work, but they are unnecessary.

Yogurt, when it's finished, behaves just about like milk. It's actually better behaved because it's impossible to curdle, sour, or clabber it. You can whip yogurt (it won't get as stiff as whipped cream), and the thicker the better for that. You can put it in the blender, beat it with a rotary beater, add all manner of things to it, cook it, all with only happy results. You can liquefy it, make it frothy, even make cheese out of it (see page 56). It is very adaptable, and if you're into natural foods, well, it's one of the most natural and most healthful you can ever find.

The only caution is this: When you cook yogurt —say, in a casserole dish or in baking bread or cake— you do destroy the yogurt bacillus and its wholesome remedial properties that can do so much good in your alimentary canal (see pages 3–5). Bearing this in mind, please go ahead and try some of the cooked dishes in this book because the flavor remains, as does the binding quality. Wherever possible, though, you should eat the soups cold or warm (not hot) and "stir in yogurt at the last minute" when making a cooked sauce.

One yogurt-fancier I know puts her milk and culture into a prewarmed thermos bottle, places the thermos on top of her television set (not too well insulated, I guess), and settles down for 4 or 5 hours of TV watching. The bacilli happily multiply away to the sound of movies of the 1930's and 1940's! Some hearty outdoor types have been known to fill their canteens or goatskin bags with milk and yogurt culture in the morning, put the bags between their bodies and their backpacks, climb a mountain, and have yogurt for supper while they watch the sun sink slowly behind the clouds in the west. Shades of the Mongol hordes (see page 2)! At least my rock-climbing friends achieve their results with the sweat of their own backs, not that of their horses.

Once you've made your first quart of home-grown yogurt, you can go on forever—just be sure not to eat any current batch up completely but to save at least ½ cup to use as a starter for the new one. Your finished yogurt will keep in the refrigerator up to 6 days; then you should use it to make fresh yogurt. I know some Armenian ladies who claim that they know a yogurt culture living in New York City that has been around for 50 years! I think that after the forty-ninth year I personally would break down and invest in a new $2 packet from the Rosell people.

Chapter 3

TEXTURES,
TEMPERATURES,
AND TANTRUMS

The ideal texture of yogurt made from whole milk is like that of smooth custard—silky and creamy to the tongue, much like the feel of sour cream or ice cream. If you start with a thinner liquid, like skin milk or watered milk, your yogurt will be thinner. In some places in this book "liquid yogurt" is specified. You can make your custardy yogurt liquid simply by stirring it or by blending it either by itself or with a thinner —water, for instance, or vegetable, chicken, or meat stock, or thin consommé. Don't be afraid of harming

11

the yogurt by whipping it in a mixer or blender; you will not destroy its health-giving properties at all.

Thick yogurt is occasionally specified in this book. If your yogurt doesn't seem thick enough, you can thicken it by adding to it some powdered milk, or if you are going to use heat, some cornstarch or some arrowroot. A bit of baking soda put into the blender with it will thicken it too. When you whip yogurt, it will never attain the stiffness of whipped cream, but whipping it together with some egg white will give you an approximation of that consistency. And of course, if you extract the liquid from yogurt, the results will have a cheesy texture, like that of cottage cheese (see page 56).

The yogurt bacilli multiply best at a temperature of between 90° and 115°, so that is the ideal warmth for *making* yogurt, but when it has reached the degree of tartness that you like, you must refrigerate it to keep it tasting that way. The temperature inside the storage part of your refrigerator (not the freezer) is perfect for preserving the yogurt. At temperatures above 120° or so, the yogurt bacilli will be killed and hence will be unable to perform all their marvelous defensive functions in your insides; but the yogurt's flavor and its binding qualities remain to give your bread, cake, or baked casserole dish its distinctive taste. As to temperatures lower than that in the storage part of your refrigerator, they too are dangerous to the life of *Bacillus bulgaricus.* That is why the dessert portion of this book shilly-shallies on the subject of freezing. For the most part, equally fine results can be obtained by *refrigerating* an ice-creamy sort of dessert rather than putting it into the freezing compartment.

If you have at some time in your cooking life switched, for example, from sugar to honey, you know that certain adjustments have to be made. (I frankly have never experienced the difficulties that some report with honey. Some cooks even recommend that you must not cook with honey until it is at least a year old!) The same is true if you have made the change from butter to margarine or vegetable butter. And if you get into the yogurt-in-place-of-milk-or-cream habit, you will soon catch on to its temperament, which is really very equable and not at all cantankerous. It may be that you will use just a bit more yogurt in any situation where you would once have used milk or cream, since it is somewhat nearer to a solid. A few experiments with sauces or with baked or sautéed dishes, however, will divulge all of yogurt's personality quirks, and you will then be friends for life. Yogurt is no prima donna!

Chapter 4

SOUPS

As the feller said, "Soup is the same as stew, only looser." (And stew, of course, is looser hash.) The soups that follow—the cold ones, anyway—if made "tighter" become dips and diet lunches. First try them loose, though with a whole-grain cracker, piece of bread, or bagel on the side. An electric blender or mixer will come in handy, but if you don't have one, a modicum of elbow grease will do the job.

14

1 ½ cups yogurt

1 tablespoon lemon juice

½ teaspoon salt

¼ teaspoon onion salt, onion powder, or finely chopped onion

1 cup shoestring or diced cooked beets

Yogurt or sour cream (optional)

Combine all ingredients except last. Stir enough to mix well or mix in a blender for a few seconds at low speed, adding the beets initially or putting them in the already-blended yogurt base. Serve chilled, with an extra dollop of yogurt (or sour cream if you're not worried about calories or cholesterol) on top. Not only delicious, but one of the handsomest and most colorful soups going.

Serves 2.

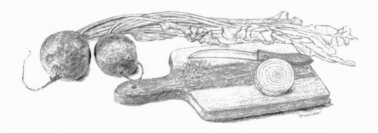

SCHAV (Sorrel Soup)

1 pint sorrel leaves (approximately)
1 tablespoon butter, margarine, or oil
2 cups water
1 cup chicken stock
1 egg, beaten lightly
1 cup yogurt
Salt or garlic salt to taste
Sour cream (optional)

If you have a garden or yard with rather acid soil, you doubtless have sorrel, a wild weed, sometimes called sour grass. It has long club-shaped leaves. Pick it, removing all sticks, stems, and blemishes, and wash it, draining it dry. Then sauté it briefly in the butter until it changes to cooked-spinach color (in fact, if you can't find any sorrel, you may substitute an equal quantity of spinach). Add it to the water and chicken stock and let it cool. When it is thoroughly cooled—or just before serving—mix in the beaten egg, yogurt, and salt. As for enhancing the soup with a dollop of sour cream, that's up to you.

Serves 4.

2 cups yogurt
1 tablespoon minced lemon rind
2 tablespoons lemon juice
2 teaspoons honey
1 egg
Dash cinnamon or nutmeg
Salt to taste
¼ cup currants or raisins

Combine all ingredients. Mix well or put in the blender and run it about 1 minute at low speed. Serve chilled. And you'll never suffer from beriberi.

Serves 4.

3 cups yogurt

1 bunch watercress

1 tablespoon minced onion

1 tablespoon minced celery (stalk and leaves) (optional)

Salt to taste

1 cup chicken or vegetable stock or consommé

Mix all the ingredients thoroughly with a spoon or in your blender. Serve chilled.

If you don't care for the rough texture, then sauté the vegetables first in a bit of oil or butter and let them cool before mixing with the yogurt, salt, and stock. (Some people would add some chopped-up dill pickle to this soup—I wouldn't.)

Serves 4.

3 cups yogurt

1 cup vegetable stock

1 cup peeled and small-cubed eggplant
(cooked or raw)

1 tablespoon minced fresh mint or 1 ½ teaspoons
dried mint

1 tablespoon minced onion

Mix all ingredients thoroughly with a spoon or in your blender. Serve chilled.

Serves 4.

CRABMEAT SOUP

This is a quick and very delicious gourmet soup made up mostly of other already-made canned soups. If you have made your own pea and tomato soups at home, so much the better, but this recipe can make the convenience soups taste like the real thing.

1 6½-ounce can crabmeat
½ cup dry sherry
2 cups yogurt
1 13-ounce can pea soup
1 13-ounce can tomato soup
Dash curry powder
Dash paprika

Soak the crabmeat in the sherry for 1 to 2 hours. Combine the remaining ingredients either by stirring or by mixing them in the blender, briefly, at low speed. Chill. Stir in the crabmeat and sherry at the last minute before serving. This can also be served warm but preferably *not* hot.

Serves 4.

SHRIMP BISQUE

2 cups yogurt
2 tablespoons lemon juice
¼ teaspoon honey
Dash dry mustard
Salt to taste
½ – ¾ cup cooked shrimp, cut up
Cold water (optional)
Cucumber, peeled or unpeeled, sliced very thin or
    diced (optional)

Combine all ingredients except last 2. Mix well or blend in the blender for a few seconds at low speed. Thin with a little cold water if it seems necessary. Some cucumber can be added before serving. Serve chilled. This could also be served warm (in which case omit the cucumber) but preferably *not* hot.

Serves 4.

AVOCADO SOUP

2 avocados
3 cups yogurt
½–¾ cup cooked chopped chicken
Salt and pepper to taste
1 lime, sliced thin and seeded

Peel avocados and remove the pits. Chop 1 up coarsely and mix in the blender with the yogurt for a few seconds at medium speed. Dice or slice the other avocado and add it to the soup, along with the chicken and seasoning. Stir well. Serve chilled, with the lime slices on top.

Serves 4.

WALNUT-CUCUMBER SOUP

3 cups yogurt
1 clove garlic, minced or pressed
2 tablespoons vegetable oil
1 cup peeled or unpeeled diced cucumber
½ teaspoon salt
1 teaspoon lemon juice
½ cup walnuts, chopped fine
1 tablespoon finely chopped parsley or snipped
    chives

Mix or blend the yogurt, garlic, and oil until smooth. Add cucumber, salt, lemon juice, and nuts. Serve chilled, with parsley or chives sprinkled on top.

Serves 4.

HAM BISQUE

---

2 cups liquid yogurt
1 cup club soda
½ cup cream
½ cup cooked smoked ham strips
Salt and pepper to taste
3–4 tablespoons chopped fresh chives

Combine the first 5 ingredients and chill. Sprinkle chives on top of the soup before serving.

Serves 4.

1 cup yogurt
3 tablespoons olive or vegetable oil
1 clove garlic, minced or pressed
1 green pepper, seeded and chopped
3–4 tomatoes, peeled and chopped
1 small cucumber, peeled and chopped
½ teaspoon cumin (or other seasoning of your
    preference)
Ice water
2 tablespoons wine or cider vinegar

Mix or blend first 7 ingredients, turning blender on and off. Add ice water a bit at a time until the soup seems the consistency you like. Stir in vinegar at last moment.

Serves 3–4.

---

1 leek or 6 scallions
3 tablespoons butter or oil
1 ripe medium-size tomato, cut up
2 cups yogurt
1 teaspoon curry powder
Salt to taste
1 teaspoon chopped chives, parsley, or dill

Sauté the leek in the butter. Add tomato, cooking it until soft. Cool, then add the yogurt, curry powder, and salt, stirring until smooth or blending briefly. Chill and serve with chives sprinkled on top.

Serves 4.

BULGARIAN SOUP

1 large onion, chopped
1 tablespoon butter or oil
1 cup yogurt
1 egg
3 cups beef bouillon or stock
Salt and pepper to taste
2 tablespoons finely chopped parsley

Sauté the onion in the butter; let it cool. Beat together the yogurt, egg, bouillon, salt, and pepper. Serve chilled, sprinkled with the parsley. (This soup may be even better served warm to hot, so decide whether you need the health-giving properties of the live yogurt more than a nice heart-warming, stomach-soothing, steaming dish.)

Serves 4.

NEW ENGLAND CLAM CHOWDER

4–5 slices bacon (or equal volume diced salt pork)
4 medium-size onions, sliced or chopped
4 medium-size potatoes (nonmealy kind), peeled
    and cut up
Water
2 cups yogurt
2 cups milk
1 pint shucked fresh clams or 1 small can chopped
    clams
Salt and pepper to taste
Butter

Sauté the bacon until quite crisp, remove from pan, and set aside. In the bacon grease cook the onions until softened. Meanwhile, parboil the potatoes in the water. Add the onions and drained potatoes to the yogurt and milk, then add the clams and their juice and the salt and pepper. Now heat the mixture (never boil) very slowly. Add the bacon, broken up into small bits (add salt pork as is), just before serving and float on the surface of each cupful or bowlful a dot of butter to melt, golden, at the last moment.

This chowder should *not* be served cold, but the traditional Yankee dish is enhanced by the taste of yogurt; so try it once in a while, forgetting about calories and cholesterol and such for that meal.

Serves 4.

2 cups yogurt
2 cups chicken or beef stock
1 cup brown or red cooked lentils
1 cup cooked barley
½ teaspoon salt
¼ teaspoon cumin

Combine all ingredients. Blend or stir together and simmer 20–30 minutes. Serve hot—or serve warm, stirring the yogurt in at the last moment.

Serves 6.

Scandinavians and some Middle Europeans are keen on fruit soups. Here's an apple soup that is fabulous —that is, if you're not turned off by the whole category.

1 pound ripe apples (approximately)
**2 tablespoons lemon juice or 1 tablespoon grated
    lemon peel**
2 cloves
2 tablespoons honey
Dash cinnamon
Water
½ cup dry white wine (optional)
2 cups yogurt

Peel the apples, core them, and cut them into chunks. Add lemon juice, cloves, honey, cinnamon, and enough water to cover. Simmer until tender, then press the fruit through a strainer or puree it in your blender, first removing the cloves. Return pureed apples to their cooking liquid. Cool mixture and add the wine and yogurt, stirring in well. Serve chilled.

Serves 4.

ANOTHER FRUIT SOUP

3 cups yogurt
1 16-ounce can fruit cocktail with its juice plus
    1 tablespoon lemon juice, or 2 cups assorted
    peeled and cut-up fresh fruit plus 1 table-
    spoon honey

Mix all ingredients thoroughly with a spoon or egg-beater or in the blender, briefly, at medium speed. Serve chilled.

Serves 4.

STILL ANOTHER FRUIT SOUP

3–5 cups yogurt
1 banana, sliced
1 pear, cored and sliced
5–6 dates, pitted and chopped
½ cup nuts, chopped
1 tablespoon maple syrup
1 teaspoon cinnamon

Mix or blend together all ingredients and serve cold.

Serves 4–6.

Chapter 5

BREADS
AND
MUFFINS

Being for some years a timid cook (or full-time office worker), I hesitated long over the baking of bread, another subject around which an aura of mystery and difficulty has floated quite undeservedly. Moreover, my head was filled with the stereotype of fresh-baked bread, smelling marvelous, coming out of the oven in a country kitchen. "Move me to the country," I said in response to my husband's importunings, "and I'll bake bread until it comes out your ears." He did. And

I did. So can you. It's very simple, and nothing impresses people with what a superb cook you are so much as the aroma of new-baked bread wafting out of the kitchen (even in the city). Here are a few bread recipes for starters, all using yogurt.

COUNTRY BREAD

2 cups milk
3 tablespoons shortening
1 tablespoon salt
4 ½ teaspoons honey
1 cup liquid yogurt
1 package active dry yeast
6–8 cups flour, sifted
Melted butter (optional)

Scald the milk and pour it over the shortening, salt, and honey and allow it to cool to lukewarm. Then stir in the yogurt and yeast (or you can add the yeast to the first cup of flour before stirring it in). Stir in the flour, 1 cup at a time, until you have a manageable dough, which means one stiff enough to knead. Knead it on a lightly floured surface for a few minutes. Then put it into a lightly greased bowl, cover it with a wet towel, and put it into a warm place to rise until it has doubled in bulk. Knead it again a bit, and divide it in half, placing each half in the greased dish in which it will bake (I usually use 2 glass baking dishes, 1 round and 1 loaf-shaped). Cover with the towel and let rise again until doubled. Bake for 50–60 minutes in a preheated 350° oven. Remove from pans to cool. You can brush the crusts with melted butter (for that shiny look) when the bread is removed from the pans if you want.

Yield: 2 medium loaves.

PAN DE AGUA

I don't know whether this is "water bread" because you bake it with water in it, under it, over it, or all three.

    1 package active dry yeast
    1 ½ cups lukewarm water
    1 cup room-temperature yogurt
    1 tablespoon salt
    1 tablespoon sugar or 1 ½ teaspoons honey
    6–8 cups flour, sifted
    Melted shortening
    Cornmeal or crushed seeds (sesame, caraway,
        sunflower)
    Water

Dissolve the yeast in the water (or stir it into the first 1 or 2 cups of flour). Add, stirring, the yogurt, salt, and sugar. Then add the flour in 3 or 4 batches, stirring it until you have quite a stiff dough. Put the dough into a lightly greased bowl, spoon some melted shortening on top of it, and cover it with a wet towel. Let it rise in a warm place until it doubles in bulk. Then on a floured surface punch it down and around a little (this bread doesn't really need much kneading) and shape it into 2 loaves of whatever shape you fancy (long or round). Lay the loaves on a cornmeal-sprinkled baking sheet. Let them sit a few minutes longer. You can take a wet knife and slash the surface of the dough if you want for a top with interesting texture. Now put the baking sheet on a rack in a cold oven with a pan of hot water on a lower rack or the bottom of the oven. Sprinkle the loaves with water and turn your oven on to 400°. Bake 40 to 50 minutes, sprinkling the loaves with water once or twice more at intervals.

This is a lovely, foolproof, crusty, shortening-free bread that may remind you of sourdough bread. It is delicious and good-looking whether it has risen a lot or only a little, so don't worry if it doesn't quite double in bulk when it rises. On the other hand, if you go away and forget it after you have shaped it into loaves and it rises again behind your back, that's all right too (it happened to me a couple of times, and the finished bread was equally tasty).

Yield: 2 medium loaves.

¾ cup finely grated cheese (sharp Cheddar, for
example)
1 tablespoon butter or margarine
2 tablespoons sugar or 1 tablespoon honey
1 teaspoon salt
1 cup lukewarm liquid yogurt
3–4 cups flour
1 package active dry yeast
2 tablespoons butter or margarine

Mix cheese, butter, sugar, and salt into yogurt and
stir until melted. Sift flour and yeast together and
add slowly to the liquid, stirring until you have a nice,
soft dough that you can knead. Knead for only 3 to
5 minutes. Let dough rise in a greased bowl, covered
with a damp towel, in a warm place until doubled in
bulk. Punch down, shape into a loaf, and put into a
greased loaf pan. Let rise again until you like the looks
of it. Melt the remaining butter, pour it on top of the
loaf, and bake about 50 minutes in a preheated 350°
oven.

Yield: 1 loaf.

3–4 cups flour

2 packages active dry yeast

1 teaspoon salt

1 tablespoon sugar or 1 ½ teaspoons honey

1 cup liquid yogurt

1 cup water

⅓ cup shortening, melted

1 egg

2 tablespoons butter or margarine, melted

Sift and mix the flour, yeast, salt, and sugar (but not the honey). Blend together the honey (if used), yogurt, water, shortening, and egg. Combine and mix well. Pat into a greased square baking pan. Cut dough into rectangles, lift out of pan, and brush cut sides with melted butter. Place rectangles on a baking sheet and allow to rise in a warm place until dough has doubled in bulk. And here's where the "speedy" comes in: Bake in a preheated 425° oven for about 20 minutes.

Yield: about 24.

BANANA BREAD

1 cup brown sugar or ½ cup honey
1 cup butter or margarine
2 eggs, lightly beaten
1 tablespoon lemon juice
2–4 bananas, mashed
½–1 cup liquid yogurt
2 cups flour
1 tablespoon baking powder
½ teaspoon salt
½ cup nutmeats, chopped (optional)

Cream sugar and butter. Mix in eggs. Stir in lemon juice, bananas, and yogurt. Sift flour, baking powder, and salt together and add, blending well. Add nuts last. Put in a greased loaf pan and bake in a preheated 350° oven for 30 minutes or so.

Being halfway between bread and cake, this is what some cookbooks would call a tea bread. In fact, it is marvelous to serve with tea, possibly spread with a bit of honey or cottage cheese or butter. I make it nearly every week because it is such a superb way to use up bananas that have begun to go overripe (for this bread, the riper the better).

Yield: 1 loaf.

½ cup ground garbanzos (chick-peas)
1 cup white or whole-wheat flour
½ teaspoon salt
½ teaspoon cinnamon
2 teaspoons baking powder
2 tablespoons powdered milk
1 cup wheat-germ or vegetable oil
½ cup brown sugar or honey
2 eggs
1 cup liquid yogurt
½ cup dates, chopped
½ cup pecans or other nuts, chopped (optional)

Mix the first 7 ingredients and the sugar, if used. Blend in another bowl the honey, if sugar isn't used, eggs, and yogurt until smooth. Stir the 2 mixtures together lightly. Add the dates and nuts last and stir just to distribute. Bake in a greased loaf pan in a preheated 375° oven for 35 to 45 minutes or until the top of the bread is nicely browned.

Yield: 1 loaf.

RAISIN LUNCHEON BREAD

2 cups any flour
4 teaspoons baking powder
½ teaspoon salt
½ cup sugar or ¼ cup honey
1 cup room-temperature liquid yogurt
2 tablespoons shortening
1 egg, lightly beaten
½ cup raisins

Topping:
½ cup brown sugar
½ teaspoon cinnamon
½ teaspoon clove
2 tablespoons butter, melted

Sift and mix first 3 ingredients and sugar, if used. Blend in another bowl the honey, if sugar isn't used, yogurt, shortening, and egg. Combine both mixtures, stirring in the raisins at the end. Pour into a greased loaf pan. Make topping by combining remaining ingredients. Pour on top of dough in pan. Bake in a preheated 350° oven for 1 hour. This is sweet enough to be called a tea bread.

Yield: 1 loaf.

2 cups flour
½ teaspoon baking soda
¼ teaspoon salt
Liquid yogurt
Melted margarine
Oil

Sift the first 3 ingredients together and add enough liquid yogurt to make a stiff dough. Knead about 5 minutes and let stand at room temperature about 20 minutes. Form into small balls about the size of an egg, then roll out about ½ inch thick. Brush melted margarine well over entire surface, fold into a ball, and roll out again. Let stand another 10 minutes, then roll out again to about ¼ inch thick. Cook on griddle, brushing with oil on both sides. Turn constantly until brown on both sides. Serve hot.

This goes very well with curry dishes (as does cold yogurt with a bit of cucumber and onion or garlic chopped into it—the way I first came to know and love yogurt).

Yield: 6 flat 6-inch-diameter breads.

Any kind of berries can be used for these muffins —blueberries being one of the most popular. If you want whole berries rather than purple streaks in your finished muffins, be sure to dust the berries with flour before putting them in.

2 cups flour
4 teaspoons baking powder
½ teaspoon salt
2 tablespoons butter or margarine
1 cup liquid yogurt
2 tablespoons honey
½ to 1 cup berries

Mix and sift the first 3 ingredients. Work in the butter with your fingertips. Add yogurt and honey; then add the berries, stirring only enough to distribute them evenly. Fill lined or lightly greased muffin cups ⅔ full and bake in a preheated 375° oven for about 20 minutes.

Yield: about 12.

CINNAMON MUFFINS

2 cups whole-wheat flour
½ cup powdered skim milk
2 teaspoons baking powder
½ teaspoon salt
1 teaspoon cinnamon
2 cups raisins
⅓ cup oil or melted margarine
½ cup honey
2 eggs
1 ½ cups yogurt
1 teaspoon vanilla extract
**Cinnamon or sugar-and-cinnamon mixture
(optional)**

Sift and mix the first 4 ingredients. Toss the cinnamon with the raisins. Mix the remaining ingredients and combine the 2 mixtures. Stir in raisins and cinnamon last, mixing only enough to distribute evenly. Fill lined or lightly greased muffin cups ⅔ full with the batter. You may sprinkle tops of muffins with additional cinnamon or a sugar-and-cinnamon mixture before baking if you wish. Bake in a preheated 350° oven for 30 minutes or so.

Yield: about 16.

1 cup yellow cornmeal
1 cup any flour
2 teaspoons baking powder
½ teaspoon salt
2 eggs
¼ cup margarine or oil
1 cup liquid yogurt
½ cup honey
1 teaspoon vanilla extract (optional)
½ cup peanut butter

Sift and mix the first 4 ingredients. Blend the next 5 ingredients. Combine the 2 mixtures. Fill lined or lightly greased muffin cups ⅔ full and bake in a pre-heated 350° oven for about 40 minutes.

This makes a delicious corn muffin. A variation with a slightly different texture and taste is made by omitting the vanilla and adding the peanut butter to the batter. Or spread the hot muffins with peanut butter instead of butter when you eat them.

Yield: 12–16.

2 cups oat or whole-wheat flour
½ teaspoon salt
½ teaspoon baking powder
½ cup softened shortening
⅓ cup liquid yogurt
¼ cup maple syrup
Butter

Sift flour, salt, and baking powder together and cut the shortening into it as if you were making pastry dough. Mix yogurt and maple syrup together and add gradually, mixing. Place dough, divided in half, in 2 lightly greased 9-inch-square baking pans and press in to fill. Mark the dough lightly to make 9 squares in each pan. Dot with butter and bake in a preheated 375° oven about 25 minutes or until firm and browned on top. Coll completely before cutting into squares. Before serving, dot with butter again and reheat.

Yield: 18.

NUT GRIDDLE CAKES

1 egg
1 cup yogurt
1 cup whole-wheat flour
½ cup white flour
½ teaspoon salt
½ teaspoon cinnamon
½ cup chopped nutmeats
Syrup (optional)

Mix all ingredients together lightly (leave some small flour lumps), then drop in spoonfuls onto a hot greased griddle. Brown on both sides and serve with syrup (if you wish).

Serves 2–4.

COTTAGE-CHEESE HOTCAKES

1 egg
6 tablespoons cottage cheese
6 tablespoons yogurt
½ teaspoon salt
2 tablespoons flour (buckwheat is nice, but any of
   your choice will do)
Syrup or powdered sugar (optional)

Mix first 4 ingredients together until smooth. Drop batter onto a hot greased griddle by spoonfuls and brown on both sides. Serve with some nice sweet syrup —maple, perhaps—or with powdered sugar or by themselves.

Serves 1 generously.

CORN PUFFS

2 cups fresh corn or 1 12-ounce can corn, drained
½ teaspoon salt
3 tablespoons liquid yogurt
2 tablespoons flour
2 eggs, separated
Oil for deep frying
Syrup or powdered sugar (optional)

Mix first 4 ingredients together, then add the egg yolks, stirring them in. Beat the egg whites until stiff, then fold them into the batter. Drop batter by spoonfuls into hot oil and brown on both sides. Serve with syrup, powdered sugar, or plain.

Serves 6.

Chapter 6

DIPS
AND
DIET LUNCHES

The thing about the imaginative little dips that you put out on your cocktail table, surrounded with things to dip into them, and diet lunches is that they are really one and the same thing—*if* your base is yogurt, that is. In the case of dips, where the evil twin sisters (cholesterol and calories) come in is in the dip*pers*; after you have exhausted the raw carrot sticks and cauliflowerets, the progression tends to be to very fatty little items: potato chips, tacos, corn chips, and the like. Whereas what you want to eat for lunch, if you are trying to be quite Spartan, is a high-protein, low-carbohydrate little job, the effects of which you try not to offset by stuffing yourself at the same time with fatty, starchy, or sugary things. Obviously, the ideal answer to this lunch problem—either in the office or at home—is a cup of yogurt to which, for variety, you have added something else both interesting and nourishing.

BUT FIRST, DIPS

And why *not* surround the dips with, instead of potato chips, raw, crisp vegetable sticks—carrot, celery, cucumber, turnip—or some thin whole-wheat crackers?

Cucumber: The most nearly ubiquitous dip of all is probably yogurt and cucumber. Chop the vegetable up into smallish dice and distribute it evenly in the yogurt. Then a topping of chives or mint. Or a sprinkling of nutmeg and/or cinnamon.

Cucumber and Something for Color: Like bits of red pimiento or green olives or black olives or yellow lemon peel or orange peel. Or blue violet petals (you can eat them—they won't hurt you). Or any of these combined.

Cucumber and Something for Zing: Finely minced raw onion, white or green, or a clove of garlic, along with the cucumber, will give a more vigorous dip. Chopped fresh dill atop this is good.

Seeds: Add to your yogurt dip a selection of seeds: sunflower, sesame, caraway, pumpkin, squash, or poppy, in combination or isolation. They pick up the dip while adding a little protein.

Avocado: Mashing up some avocado in equal quantity to yogurt makes a lovely-looking, nourishing dip. Add a dash of lemon or lime juice.

Avocado Plus: To the above add some shredded sharp cheese (or cream in some blue cheese). Then some chili powder or cayenne pepper or Tabasco sauce.

Nuts: Walnuts, pecans, peanuts, filberts, cashews, chestnuts, Brazil nuts, pistachios, macadamias—practically any nut whose flavor you like, broken up and stirred into the yogurt, makes a fine dip. Particularly if you surround it with destringed celery stalks.

Water Chestnuts and Lotus Root: These 2 exotic crunchies, thinly sliced, go well in your yogurt dip. If you don't live near a Chinese (or other Far Eastern) market, fresh raw turnips can substitute.

Peanut Butter: It may sound a bit alarming (especially to those who make a fetish of *hating* peanut butter), but try mixing a spoonful of peanut butter (or any other nut butter you may have created with your blender or mortar and pestle) into your yogurt dip. Try it with apple chunks added as well.

Soybean Mash: Mashed cooked soybeans make a tasty spread or dip when combined with yogurt.

Chick-pea Mash: And so do mashed cooked chick-peas. Especially if you add one of those envelopes of onion-soup or -dip mixture.

Caviar: A chic Washington, D.C., hostess I know always mixes yogurt with red caviar for a predinner dip.

HUMMOS

A Middle Eastern dip.

> 1 17-ounce can chick-peas (garbanzos)
> 1 clove garlic, pressed
> 1 teaspoon salt
> ½ cup lemon juice
> ½ cup yogurt
> ½ cup sesame paste (optional)

Mash chick-peas with their liquid in your blender or with your strong right hand. Then add other ingredients and blend again. You may sprinkle a bit of vegetable oil and a bit of some chopped herbs or greens over the top before you put it out on your table.

6 eggs, hard-cooked, cut in half lengthwise

2–3 tablespoons soft butter or margarine

½ cup yogurt

1 teaspoon Worcestershire sauce

Salt, pepper, and paprika to taste

Pinch dry mustard

1 tablespoon chopped parsley (or other herbs of
   your choice)

Remove egg yolks from whites and cream them with remaining ingredients, then spoon the mixture back into the hollows of the whites. You may want to garnish with some bits of shredded meat, fish, nuts, olives, or seeds.

Or if you are in the cholesterol worry-bag, then for egg yolks substitute powdered skim milk and color the stuffing mixture with some saffron. What will you do with the egg yolks? Let a fearless friend use them in eggs à la goldenrod.

CLAM DIP

1 6½-ounce can minced clams
1 4-ounce package cream cheese
2–3 tablespoons yogurt
2 teaspoons chopped onion
1 teaspoon soy sauce
Dash Tabasco sauce

Drain clams (drink the liquid mixed with cranberry juice). Combine thoroughly with remaining ingredients and chill.

Is your imagination now stimulated enough in the department of dip, spread, or sandwich filling? If so, let's go back to the subject of diet lunches.

NOW DIET LUNCHES

Many are the white- or blue-collar workers—many more every day—who, if not expense-account feeding that day, make a lunch of a container of commercial yogurt—plain, vanilla, or some fruit flavor (strawberry still seems to be the all-time favorite in the East). If you lunch at home, you can keep your figure by following the very same program. You don't even have to run out to the supermarket or delicatessen and purchase that waxy carton if you have made up your week's supply of yogurt at home (pages 6–10). You have only to spoon out a bowlful of that creamy white, clean-tasting stuff and peer into the pantry or refrigerator to see what you can add to it.

Adding Fruit

One of the best goodies you can make with a twist of the wrist is yogurt and applesauce, with or without that extra bit of sugar (date sugar, for example) or syrup. Or add a seasoning like cinnamon.

You may have 1 leftover serving of cranberry sauce which needn't wait until the next poultry dinner; stir it in.

Or stir in ½ can of peaches, pears, raspberries, blue-berries, prunes, or plums; or a handful of boysenberries; or a bit of guava, papaya, or mango.

Is there only 1 banana left after the departure of the cereal-eaters this morning? Slice it up and throw in a few currants.

That 1 cupful of canned (diet?) fruit cocktail isn't going far toward tomorrow's party dessert. Throw it into your yogurt cup.

The addition of crushed pineapple (to which you've added some chopped prunes) makes a popular yogurt lunch. (To me it is a bit redundant, since the flavors of pineapple and yogurt are too similar. I prefer more contrast, such as yogurt and stewed rhubarb.)

Some figs and dates, cut into small chunks, can turn a cup of plain (or vanilla) yogurt into a lunch fit for royalty.

Some dried (or fresh) apricots or peaches?

Adding Vegetables (or Fish or Eggs)

In searching for that component of the perfect diet lunch, don't stop at the fruits. What vegetables have you in your root cellar or refrigerator which you can combine, either raw or cooked, with yogurt for your varied diet lunches?

One of the most delicious (pretty too) eat-on-the-train lunches I've ever toted was created from bits of leftover-from-the-night-before wax beans and artichoke hearts, plus a sprinkling of cress from my greenhouse.

How about taking the vegetable peeler and shaving some carrot curls into your yogurt bowl, together with some raw-beet shavings and a leaf of lettuce, cut up small?

Do you find on the second shelf only 1 serving of cooked yellow squash or broccoli or Brussels sprouts? Plop it into your cup of yogurt and marvel.

Or what's the matter with simple little old green peas, snap beans, spinach? And if you cooked them with some slivered almonds last night, so much the better.

One of the best surprises for me occurred when I found less than a serving of eggplant *parmigiana* and stirred *that* into my lunchtime yogurt. Ambrosia!

Leftover herbed rice—½ cup—was another.

And about ⅔ cup mushrooms, cooked but then left out of the dish at the last moment the night before (remembering that my husband is not fond of mushrooms and that nowhere is it written that they *must* go into any meat and vegetable casserole), was a third.

Some asparagus tips in butter make your yogurt a king's luncheon.

On an especially hot day cut up into your diet lunch bowl a couple of radishes and a few leaves of endive.

And on a day when you aren't surfeited with fish, stir in some flakes of tuna, 1 or 2 sardines (with or without hard-cooked egg), or a few cross sections of pickled herring.

"Cottage Cheese"

A vigorous senior citizen I know never eats anything for lunch but a cup of cottage cheese (sometimes decorated with a bit of fresh fruit or some berries), and for all I know, her ilk may be legion. She feels that this allows her the stevedore's repast that is her usual breakfast, a gourmand's dinner—and a healthy old age. If this seems a sound plan to you, why not make your own cottage cheese?

Just spoon a quantity of yogurt (you might as well start with 1 quart) into a jelly bag (if you lack a jelly bag, fashion one with a drawstring top out of a few thicknesses of cheesecloth). Hang it up (possibly suspended from a faucet) over your kitchen sink overnight. When you get up the next morning, open the bag and scrape out your new homemade "cottage cheese."

It will be, of course, yogurt curds (from which the whey, or liquid, has dripped out), its consistency and even taste loosely related to cottage cheese, or farmer cheese, and *feta* (Greek sheep's-milk cheese). You may want to eat it just as it is, or you can add some flavorings to it—vanilla or wine or your favorite seasonings and herbs. Have it for lunch or serve it on crackers or as a dip.

One of the dangers of the yogurt diet lunch may be that it leaves you feeling the need for something really crunchable to nibble with it. Understandable. But stay away from the potato-chip bag, the store-boughten white-bread toast, and the redoubtable corn-cheese products. Accompany your diet lunch bowl with a few rye crackers or their whole-grain relatives instead. They will satisfy your chewing urge without filling up your veins with cholesterol or your midsection with fatty deposits.

Chapter 7

SALAD DRESSINGS AND SAUCES

If you are devoted to mayonnaise and have grown up on one of the commercial brands, the first thing you ought to know is that at the dawning of the American consciousness that we were poisoning ourselves little by little through our heavy use of convenience foods, for some reason mayonnaise and salad dressing were exempted from the requirement that all ingredients be listed on the jar label. So you just have no idea of the weird and worrisome elements that go into the commercially prepared versions of these foods as colorings, preservatives, and so on.

The easy suggestion that can be made to a commercial-mayonnaise devotee, therefore, is simply to substitute yogurt for mayonnaise in all the places where you would slather on that old stuff: on a tomato-and-cucumber salad, on the bread that would have received a basting of mayonnaise before you lay on the tuna fish, the chopped-egg salad, the watercress and cucumber, or the ham and cheese.

And here are some salad dressings made with a base of yogurt which will go very well with nearly any green salad or can serve as sauces for hot or cold vegetables:

1 cup yogurt
2 tablespoons chopped chives
1 tablespoon capers
1 teaspoon lemon juice

1 cup yogurt
1 clove garlic, minced or pressed
1 tablespoon minced parsley

1 cup yogurt
2 tablespoons chili sauce or piccalilli
1 tablespoon catsup or tomato sauce

1 cup yogurt
½ cup finely grated Cheddar, Parmesan, Romano,
    or other fairly sharp cheese

1 cup yogurt

½ cup chopped celery (leaves especially)

½ teaspoon honey

½ teaspoon pressed garlic or 1 teaspoon finely
    chopped onion

1 cup yogurt

1 tablespoon dried oregano

1 teaspoon dried basil or thyme

1 cup yogurt

1 tablespoon fresh fennel leaves (or 1 teaspoon
    dried)

1 teaspoon mustard

1 cup yogurt

1–2 egg yolks, raw or hard-cooked

1–2 tablespoons lemon juice

(This one will give you more the color of your old
favorite mayonnaise.)

1 cup yogurt

½ cup wheat-germ or vegetable oil

1 tablespoon lemon juice

½ teaspoon salt or garlic salt

1 cup yogurt

6–8 anchovies, chopped

1 tablespoon chopped scallions

Here are some dressings that are probably better on fruit salads of one kind or another:

1 cup yogurt
1 tablespoon mint jelly or fresh mint leaves or
    1 ½ teaspoons dried mint

1 cup yogurt
1 tablespoon chopped pimiento
1 tablespoon chopped pitted green olives

1 cup yogurt
1 tablespoon chopped pitted black olives
1 tablespoon juice from a jar of sweet pickles

1 cup yogurt
1 tablespoon almond extract
1 cup mashed banana

1 cup yogurt
½ cup crushed raspberries or 2 tablespoons rasp-
    berry syrup or the juice from frozen berries

1 cup yogurt
2 tablespoons chopped maraschino cherries
1 tablespoon grated orange peel

1 cup yogurt
1 tablespoon powdered milk
2–3 tablespoons liquid from a jar of green olives

And here are some sauces that will enhance meats or fish. (If you wonder how we get from salad dressings to sauces, it's very simple: They are constitutionally much the same, the only distinction being in the head of the person who thinks of a sauce as runnier. If you are such a person, be sure your yogurt for sauces is less thick, nearer to liquid.)

1 cup yogurt
1 teaspoon Worcestershire sauce
1 teaspoon dry mustard
1 teaspoon grated onion, shallot, or garlic

1 cup yogurt
1 tablespoon dry mustard
1 tablespoon grated horseradish

1 cup yogurt
1 tablespoon chopped fresh dill (or 1 teaspoon dried)
1–2 tablespoons seeds, such as anise, caraway, or sesame (alone or in combination)

1 cup yogurt
1 tablespoon melted butter
½ cup fine bread crumbs
1 tablespoon Worcestershire sauce
Splash of bitters

1 cup yogurt
1 tablespoon cider or wine vinegar
2 tablespoons chopped onion
Dash cayenne pepper

1 cup yogurt
1–2 tablespoons tomato sauce
2 tablespoons cottage cheese

1 cup yogurt
3 tablespoons crushed pineapple
1 tablespoon curry powder

This one especially for cold fish or aspic:

1 cup yogurt
1 teaspoon garlic juice
2 teaspoons anchovy paste
3 tablespoons very finely chopped black olives

And this for ham:

1 jar apple jelly, melted
1 cup yogurt
¼ teaspoon cloves
2 tablespoons tarragon vinegar

And this for lamb:

Pour out the fat from the pan in which you have roasted your lamb. Deglaze pan over high heat with ¾ cup white wine. Cool and add:

1 tablespoon finely chopped dill pickle
1 tablespoon capers
2 tablespoons butter
1 teaspoon dried tarragon
Salt and pepper to taste
½ cup yogurt

Chapter 8

GOURMET
VEGETABLE
TREATS

Entirely respectable, even morally attractive, is the
trend toward vegetarianism enjoying a renascence in
this country today. It is variously defined as eating
no flesh or animal product, allowing only fish and seafood into your otherwise plant diet, including only
eggs and poultry, eating eggs but not the flesh of the
creature that produces them. If you are into a vegetarian diet of some kind or thinking of getting into
one, study this chapter carefully (and skip the following one). Although yogurt (a once-removed animal

product) is present in every recipe, none includes any flesh. And they will allay any fears you may have that being a vegetarian is synonymous with going hungry; these are all soul- and stomach-satisfying dishes.

ASPARAGUS ASTOUNDING

½ pound asparagus
Water
½–1 cup mushrooms, chopped
3–4 tablespoons chopped onion
Oil or butter
½ cup bread crumbs (or ¼ cup bread crumbs,
    ¼ cup Bacos)
½ cup yogurt
1 tablespoon wheat-germ oil
1 tablespoon minced parsley
Salt and pepper to taste
Pinch turmeric
½ cup grated Cheddar cheese (optional)

Cook asparagus (steaming or simmering it) with water until *al dente*. Sauté mushrooms and onion in oil. Drain asparagus and lay them in a lightly greased baking dish. Mix all the ingredients but the last together and pour over the asparagus. Sprinkle the grated cheese (if you wish) over the top. Bake in a preheated 350° oven for about 20 minutes.

Serves 4–6.

6 white turnips
1 tablespoon caraway seeds
Salt
Water
½ cup yogurt
½ teaspoon dried basil
½ teaspoon honey
Paprika (optional)

Simmer the turnips and caraway seeds in slightly salted water for about 10 minutes. Drain, cool, slice, and lay in a lightly greased baking dish. Add the yogurt, basil, and honey. Sprinkle with paprika (if desired) —or sprinkle with paprika just before serving. Bake 25 to 35 minutes in a preheated 350° oven.

The surprise in this dish is that turnips were my least-favorite vegetable, with the possible exception of parsnips, until I prepared them this way. The surprise when I prepared them for a still-doubting Thomas was that Tom won't eat anything with caraway seeds in it—they get in his teeth. Even this objection could be removed if you ground the caraway seeds into a powder.

Serves 4–6.

ZUCCHINI CASSEROLE

**About 1 pound zucchini, sliced (or summer squash
 or eggplant)**
Salt
Water
1 garlic clove, pressed or minced
3 tablespoons butter or margarine
1 cup canned drained chick-peas
½ pound green tomatoes, chopped or sliced
2 tablespoons flour or arrowroot
1 cup yogurt
½ cup bread crumbs (optional)

Cook the zucchini in boiling salted water until nearly tender. Drain and reserve the cooking liquid. Brown the garlic in the butter, then add chick-peas and cook 5 minutes longer. Add green tomatoes and cook 5 minutes more. Stir in the flour and cook long enough to thicken. Add cooked zucchini and about ½ cup of the cooking liquid, cooking and stirring a few minutes longer. Stir in the yogurt just before serving. If you add bread crumbs to the top, do so at the last moment, browning a few moments under the broiler if you wish.

Serves 4–6.

RED FLANNEL HASH

This is a good way, and a traditional one, to use up leftover beets and potatoes.

> Cooked beets
> Cooked potatoes
> Yogurt
> Salt, pepper, and other spices to taste

Chop or mash up all the ingredients together, put into a buttered baking dish, and bake in a preheated 350° oven for 20 to 30 minutes. (Some people would serve this with a soft-cooked egg on top. I wouldn't.)

EGGPLANT CURRY

> 2 teaspoons salt
> 1 large eggplant, peeled and diced
> ¼ cup butter or margarine
> 1 medium onion, minced
> 1 clove garlic, minced or pressed
> 1–2 teaspoons curry powder
> ½ cup chopped pimiento, or pimiento strips
> (optional)
> 1 cup yogurt

Salt the eggplant, then sauté in covered pan in the butter until tender. Remove eggplant. Add onion, garlic, curry powder, and pimiento, if desired, to the pan (or lay the pimiento strips on top when serving) and heat through. Combine with eggplant. Cool the dish to room temperature and stir in the yogurt just before serving.

Serves 4.

FANCY CORN PUDDING

1 16-ounce can corn kernels and their liquid
2 carrots, shredded
1 green onion, minced (or 3 tablespoons chopped chives)
2 eggs, lightly beaten
1 cup yogurt
½ cup toasted wheat germ or 3 tablespoons wheat-germ oil
Pinch tarragon or oregano
Salt to taste

Blend all ingredients together. Pour into a lightly greased pan and bake in a preheated 350° oven for 40 to 45 minutes.

Serves 4–6.

2–3 tablespoons oil or melted margarine
2 stalks celery with leaves, chopped
1 clove garlic, pressed or minced
2 cups cut-up tomatoes
1½ cups mashed potatoes
1 pound brown lentils, cooked (in 3 cups water and
    1 tablespoon soy sauce), or baby lima beans,
    cooked
1 cup yogurt
1 teaspoon thyme or basil
Salt and pepper to taste

In half the oil sauté the celery, and when it's softened, the garlic. Add the tomatoes, and sauté them. Combine with the remaining ingredients and put into a casserole dish. Bake for 30 minutes in a preheated 350° oven.

Serves 4–6.

4 large green peppers
Oil
½ cup chopped onion
1 cup diced celery (stalk and leaves)
¾ cup sliced mushrooms
¾ cup artichoke hearts
½ cup yogurt
½ cup tomato sauce
1 teaspoon fresh chopped dill
Salt to taste
A few pine nuts (optional)

Hollow out the peppers and reserve. Heat a little oil and sauté the onion and celery until softened. Add mushrooms and artichoke hearts and sauté a bit longer. Then add the rest of the ingredients, cool, and stuff the peppers with the mixture. Oil the outsides of the peppers and bake in a preheated 350° oven for 30 to 45 minutes.

These peppers are unusual because the usual thing to stuff peppers with is a mixture of meat, rice, and onions. You can also use this stuffing for cabbage leaves or grape leaves, if you prefer, instead of peppers. In that case I recommend simmering the stuffed leaves covered, on top of the stove, in a little stock, rather than baking.

Serves 2–4.

2 avocados
1 cup bean sprouts
2–3 tablespoons minced onion
3–4 tablespoons finely diced celery
½ cup yogurt
1 tablespoon lime juice
½ teaspoon powdered ginger

Halve the avocados and remove pits. Remove the avocado flesh from the skin halves without tearing them, cut flesh into small dice, and mix with all the other ingredients. Put mixture into the avocado shells. Then if you don't like the looks of it, sprinkle some contrasting color of dressing or spice over the top— or some sunflower or sesame seeds.

Serves 4.

Brown rice must be cooked somewhat longer than white rice, but of course, it is worth it, as nearly all the nutrients are polished off white rice and nearly all are retained by brown rice, a good source of protein.

2 garlic cloves, pressed
2 tablespoons chopped green pepper
1 medium onion, chopped
Oil
1 cup brown rice, cooked until nearly soft
1–2 cups bean sprouts or water chestnuts (or both)
1–2 cups chopped cooked broccoli
½–1 teaspoon saffron
Pinch fresh or dried thyme or basil
½ cup yogurt

Sauté the garlic, pepper, and onion in a little oil until softened. Add the rice, vegetables, saffron, and thyme and sauté until the rice begins to get crisp. Stir in yogurt just before serving.

Serves 4.

SOYBEAN LOAF

1 cup cooked soybeans
1–2 tablespoons chopped onion
½ cup chopped celery (with leaves)
Oil or butter
½ cup grated carrots
1 cup liquid yogurt
1 cup vegetable stock
½ cup tomato sauce
Salt and pepper to taste

Mash the soybeans. Sauté onion and celery in oil until softened. Combine with remaining ingredients. (The amount of liquid may sound like a lot for a "loaf," but the soybeans absorb a good deal.) Bake in a lightly oiled loaf pan for 45 minutes in a preheated 350° oven.

Serves 4–6.

Actually, some of these vegetables may be more orange than yellow; the taste will in any case be golden on the palate.

> **About 3 cups acorn squash, butternut squash, pumpkin, and yam or sweet potato**
> **1 cup yogurt**
> **2–3 tablespoons butter or margarine**
> **Salt, pepper, and nutmeg to taste**
> **½ cup slivered almonds**
> **½ cup shredded Cheddar or Swiss cheese (with or without bread crumbs mixed in)**

Slice the vegetables quite thin and distribute them in a buttered baking dish. Dot with yogurt, butter, salt, pepper, nutmeg, and almonds, top with cheese, and bake about 40 minutes in a preheated 350–375° oven.

Some white potato mixed in (if you don't mind the tweed effect) would not be amiss. As long as the combination of vegetables includes butternut squash (and it's of a good quality), the taste will knock you out.

Serves 4–6.

4–5 large onions, sliced

3–4 green peppers, seeded, pith removed, and
    sliced

Oil or margarine

3 garlic cloves, minced

2 16-ounce cans peeled tomatoes with their liquid

2 16-ounce cans red kidney beans with their liquid

Salt and pepper to taste

2–3 tablespoons chili powder

1 cup room-temperature yogurt

Sauté the onions and peppers in a little oil, adding garlic at end. Then mix with everything else (some people would drain the beans, but it is not necessary) except yogurt and simmer, covered, on top of your stove for an hour or so. Stir in the yogurt at the last moment, just before serving.

(If you prefer your chili *con carne,* add cooked meat—browned chopped beef, veal, or pork or a combination—before simmering. And in that case you could also add browned bacon bits and sauté the vegetables in the bacon grease instead of oil or margarine.)

Serves 6–8.

SPINACH QUICHE

1 pie crust, unbaked
1 tablespoon chopped onion
1 cup shredded cheese (Swiss, Cheddar, Gruyère,
    or Parmesan)
2 eggs, lightly beaten
1 cup yogurt
1 tablespoon flour or arrowroot
Salt and pepper to taste
Pinch nutmeg
1 cup cooked chopped spinach

Bake the pie crust in a preheated 450° oven for 10 minutes. Sprinkle onion and cheese over the crust. Blend together the eggs, yogurt, flour, salt and pepper, and nutmeg. Stir in the spinach to distribute it evenly. Pour this mixture over the onions and cheese and put into the 450° oven on the lowest rack. After 15 minutes reduce heat to 350° and bake about 30 minutes longer.

Serves 6–8.

2 cups partially cooked *basmatti* rice
½ cup ghee or clarified butter
Water
1 tablespoon saffron
2 tablespoons pistachio nuts
1 teaspoon black mustard seeds
Ghee or clarified butter
1 teaspoon *garam masala* (a spice mix)
8–10 carrots, cut up
2 cups peas
1 head of cauliflower, cut up small
1 teaspoon cumin
1 teaspoon sea salt
2 cups yogurt

Sauté the rice in the ghee until golden, being careful not to burn it. Then cook rice in a pot of boiling water, adding saffron and pistachio nuts, until rice is nearly soft. Meanwhile, sauté the mustard seeds in a small amount of ghee until they pop. Add *garam masala.* When the mixture is hot, add the carrots, peas, and cauliflower, stirring constantly for about 15 minutes. Grease a baking dish and spread the rice mixture, drained of any excess liquid, on the bottom. Then add the vegetables and ghee mixture in a second layer. Add cumin and salt to yogurt and top the vegetables with it. Cover casserole with waxed paper without touching yogurt, cover waxed paper with several thicknesses of cheesecloth, and tie all in place. Bake 50–60 minutes in a preheated 325° oven. Turn out carefully so that the glazed rice is on top. Serve in wedges.

Serves 10–12.

SPROUT SALAD

1 ½ cups alfalfa and lentil sprouts
2 medium-size organic tomatoes
1 cup yogurt
1 tablespoon soy sauce
1 teaspoon sea salt

Mix all ingredients together and serve cold.

Serves 4–6.

CARROT-RAISIN SALAD

2 pounds carrots, shredded
1 cup Monukka raisins
2 cups yogurt
Sea kelp (optional)
Lemon juice (optional)

Mix the first 3 ingredients together and season (if desired) with the last 2. Serve cold.

Serves 4–6.

Chapter 9

GOURMET
FEASTS,
NONVEGETARIAN

If you are a nonreconstructed gourmet who still thinks that to eat really superbly is to dine on the flesh of fish, fowl, or mammal, then perhaps you will enjoy some of the following yogurt-invested dishes.

CHICKEN IN OYSTER SAUCE

1 onion, minced
3–4 tablespoons butter or margarine
1 garlic clove, pressed or minced
½ cup flour or arrowroot
1 cup yogurt
2 cups chicken stock or combination of chicken
    stock and liquid from oysters
1 teaspoon fresh or dried thyme or oregano
Salt and pepper to taste
½ teaspoon honey (optional)
1 pint fresh or thawed frozen shucked oysters,
    drained
1 chicken (cut in serving pieces) or 2 whole chicken
    breasts, cooked
½ cup buttered bread crumbs
½ cup grated cheese

Sauté the onion in the butter until golden, adding the garlic at the end. Stir in the flour and then the yogurt, slowly, until mixture thickens. Now add stock, thyme, salt and pepper, and honey (if desired) and bring the sauce to a boil. Then simmer it 5 minutes. Add oysters (chopped, if you wish, or whole) and simmer another 3 or 4 minutes. Place chicken in a baking dish and pour sauce over. Sprinkle with crumbs and cheese and bake in a preheated 375° oven for 20 to 30 minutes.

Serves 4–6.

SEAFOOD CURRY

1 pound fresh or frozen shrimp or other seafood
Salt
Water
¼ cup butter or margarine
¼ cup flour or arrowroot
2 cups liquid yogurt
1 teaspoon curry powder (or more, depending on
     how strong you like your curry)
2–3 bananas, sliced
Hot cooked rice
2 tablespoons chopped parsley

Simmer shrimp in salted water until they turn opaque. Drain, cool, and shell and devein them. Melt the butter and stir in the flour to make a paste. Add yogurt, stirring constantly until mixture is thickened. Stir in curry powder. Stir the bananas into the sauce. When they have softened a bit, put in the shrimp and cook just long enough to heat through. Serve on rice with parsley sprinkled on top.

Serves 6–8.

1 cup flaked fish (such as canned tuna or salmon;
   cooked flounder, perch, sole, mackerel)
1 cup seasoned bread cubes
1 egg, beaten
1 cup yogurt
½ cup sliced mushrooms
2 tablespoons minced onion
½ cup minced celery (stalk and leaves)
Pinch salt
Sliced pitted olives and/or pimiento, or a sauce of
   your choice (optional)

Line the bottom of a loaf pan with wax paper. Combine all ingredients except last and pour into pan. Bake in a preheated 350° oven for 45–50 minutes. Cool 5 to 10 minutes before turning out onto a platter. Then you can decorate the top with olives and/or pimiento if you wish. Or serve the loaf with a sauce.

Serves 4–6.

The virtue of this dish is that it's a good and tasty way to get some liver into someone who needs the iron but doesn't care much for plain liver. And you can save money at the same time because you don't have to use calves' liver.

> 1 pound beef liver
> Seasoned flour
> 3–4 onions, sliced
> 3 tablespoons oil
> 1 garlic clove, pressed or minced
> ¼ cup butter or margarine
> 3–4 tablespoons flour, cornstarch, or arrowroot
> 1 cup yogurt
> 1 cup beer
> ½ cup vegetable stock
> Hot cooked rice or noodles
> Chopped herbs or green (optional)

Clean and cut liver (with scissors) into 1-inch pieces. Dredge them in flour. Sauté onions in oil until golden, remove, and keep warm. Brown the garlic in the oil, then turn the heat high and brown the liver on both sides quickly. Remove liver and keep warm. Lower heat, then add butter and flour to the pan, stirring until pasty. Add yogurt, beer, and stock. Bring it to a simmer and cook, stirring, until thickened. Return onions and meat to pan and cook another minute or so. Serve warm over noodles or rice. You can add some chopped herbs to the top if you wish, mostly for color.

Serves 4–6.

This is a Middle Eastern dish with infinite variations, mostly in the seasoning and sauce. It usually includes lamb and eggplant.

> 1 medium eggplant
> Salt
> 1 stick butter or margarine
> ¾ pound lamb, ground or finely chopped
> 1 medium onion, finely chopped
> Salt and pepper to taste
> ½ cup tomato sauce
> 3–4 tablespoons chopped parsley
> ½ cup yogurt
> ½ cup grated cheese (optional)

Slice eggplant crosswise in pieces about ½ inch thick. Sprinkle eggplant with salt and set aside for ½ hour or so. In 1 tablespoon of butter sauté the meat until brown. Add onion and cook until golden. Season to taste with salt and pepper. Add tomato sauce and parsley and cook a bit longer. Now rinse the salt off the eggplant, pat dry, and brown the eggplant in the rest of the butter. Stir the yogurt into the meat mixture. Arrange eggplant and meat mixture in alternate layers in a baking dish and top with the cheese. Bake in a preheated 375° oven for 30 to 40 minutes.

Serves 4–6.

This is traditionally made with beef but works fine with veal.

1–1 ½ pounds beef or veal (a good cut)
Salt and pepper to taste
3–4 tablespoons margarine
1 tablespoon flour or arrowroot
1 cup beef stock
1 large onion, sliced or chopped
1 teaspoon mustard
½ cup yogurt
Hot cooked rice, noodles, potatoes, or polenta
(optional)

Trim the meat and cut it into cubes or strips. You can season the meat now and let it sit or season the sauce later. Melt 1½ tablespoons margarine in a saucepan and stir in the flour to make a paste. Preheat the stock and add it to the saucepan, whisking until the mixture thickens and is smooth. Keep it warm. Melt the rest of the margarine separately and brown the onion in it. Then either throw away the onion or leave it in the pan and add the meat, browning it on both sides—cook it only long enough to brown, not to toughen. Now stir the mustard and yogurt into the sauce, pour it over the meat (and onions?) and serve warm. It is good over rice or noodles or potatoes or polenta or all by itself.

Serves 4–6.

¼ cup minced onion

3 tablespoons margarine

About 1 ½ pounds ground meat (a combination of
     beef, veal, and pork is traditional)

1 egg, beaten

Seasonings to taste

Bread crumbs or cubes (optional)

Stock or water (optional)

½ cup flour

1 tablespoon arrowroot

1 cup yogurt

2–3 tablespoons soy sauce

Hot cooked rice or noodles

Sauté onion in 2 tablespoons of the margarine in a frying pan until golden (or leave it raw if you prefer). Remove the onion and combine with the meat, egg, seasonings, bread (if you want to fill out the meat and cheat a little), and some liquid to moisten if it seems to need it. Now make balls of about golf-ball size. Taking a few at a time, dredge them in the flour (a good way to do this is to shake the flour and meatballs together inside a paper bag). Now brown the meatballs in the margarine in the frying pan, a few at a time, shaking them around to brown them all over and keep them round. Remove and keep them warm. Put the arrowroot and the other tablespoon of the margarine into a saucepan and whisk it to make a paste.

Then preheat the yogurt and soy sauce and add to the pan, whisking until mixture is thick and smooth. Pour over meatballs and serve with rice or noodles.

Serves 6–8.

TURKEY SALAD

Here is a good and handsome method of doing in leftover turkey or other fowl.

    2 cups cubed cooked turkey meat
    2 stalks celery and leaves, chopped
    1 medium onion, chopped
    1 cup seedless grapes
    1 cup melon balls (cantaloupe, for color, would be
        good)
    ½ cup toasted almonds
    1 cup yogurt
    1 teaspoon cumin or cayenne pepper
    Lettuce

Just mix together all ingredients but the last and serve cold either in individual servings on leaves of green or in a large salad bowl lined with lettuce first.

Serves 4–6.

2 tablespoons cornstarch or arrowroot

½ cup butter or margarine, melted

½–1 cup canned tomatoes with their liquid

1 cup liquid yogurt

A bit of stock (if necessary)

1 ½ teaspoons powdered ginger

1 teaspoon chili powder

1 cup chopped nuts

½ cup raisins (optional)

3 tablespoons coconut shreds

1 duck, cooked, boned, and cubed

Mix the cornstarch with the melted butter over low heat until a paste forms. Then add tomatoes, yogurt, and stock, continuing to stir until the mixture thickens and is smooth. Add ginger, chili powder, nuts, raisins, and coconut and cook a bit longer. Then pour over duck and put in a preheated 325° oven until everything is warmed through, or you can add the duck to the sauce and stir for a few minutes until the meat is heated.

There is no reason why this couldn't be Indian chicken or turkey or squab. Or if your vegetarianism has developed that far, omit the *carne* entirely, add some strips of green pepper and some mushrooms, and serve the dish over rice or noodles.

Serves 6–8.

A surprising and delightful flavor combination.

- 1 ½ pounds chicken livers
- 1 tablespoon oil or butter
- 1 8-ounce can tangerine or mandarin-orange sections, or pineapple chunks, with their liquid
- 1 6-ounce can baby white onions
- 2–3 tomatoes, cut up
- ½ cup sliced pitted green or black olives
- Few slices pimiento
- 1 tablespoon soy sauce
- 1 cup yogurt
- 2 tablespoons lime juice
- Pinches of fresh or dried mint, basil, marjoram
- 1 cup dry white wine or stock

Brown the livers quickly in the oil and remove. Then mix everything else together. (Alternately, the yogurt may be left out of the sauce [in that case use more liquids in it] and spooned over the dish when you take it out of the oven.) Pour the sauce over the livers in a baking dish, and bake in a preheated 350° oven for 30 minutes.

Serves 6.

6 pork chops
Salt and pepper to taste (optional)
3 tablespoons butter or margarine
3–4 tablespoons minced green onion
1 cup thick yogurt
½ teaspoon cayenne pepper
1 teaspoon paprika
1 teaspoon mustard

Sprinkle the pork chops with salt and pepper (or omit them in favor of the other seasonings). Brown chops in half the butter on both sides, cooking them until they are nearly as done as you like them; keep them warm. Melt the rest of the butter and sauté the green onion in it until golden. Add ½ cup yogurt, cayenne, paprika, and mustard and cook a bit longer. Then when you have removed this sauce from heat, stir in the other ½ cup yogurt. Serve sauce warm over chops.

Serves 6.

---

6 portions lamb (chops or cutlets)
Margarine or oil
2–3 tablespoons water
½ pound whole small mushrooms
12 juniper berries (approximately)
Salt and pepper to taste
Rosemary or thyme (fresh or dried)
Oregano (fresh or dried)
1 teaspoon cornstarch
½ cup dry vermouth (optional)
½ cup yogurt

Brown the lamb on both sides in margarine. Add water, cover pan, and simmer 15 minutes. Remove chops and keep warm. Add mushrooms, juniper berries, salt and pepper, rosemary, and oregano and continue simmering about 15 minutes more. Stir in cornstarch and stir until smooth. Add vermouth (if desired) and cook for a minute or so. Remove from heat, stir in yogurt, pour over chops, and serve.

Serves 6.

Chapter 10

DRINKS

Liquid yogurt is achieved simply by stirring up your yogurt with a spoon until the pudding-like texture breaks down and it is thin and smooth or liquid. Or of course, you can liquefy it by adding water, milk, or some other liquid first and then stirring. You can make it fully liquid—and drinkable—in just a few seconds in a blender or with a rotary beater or wire whisk. For delicious cool drinks you can combine yogurt with things that have an ice base, and with a little stirring, you'll soon have a bibbable potion.

Following are some suggestions for yogurt drinks. Unless otherwise specified, each is measured in terms of 1 tall (or 2 short) glasses. Multiplication is very simple if you want to serve 2 or more people who drink long.

GAYELORD HAUSER SPECIAL

Mr. Hauser was one of the daddies of the health-food movement that is today so favored by the younger generation. He claimed that with the following 3 ingredients alone, man would banish most of his ills and live to a ripe and vigorous old age.

1 cup yogurt
1 tablespoon blackstrap molasses
1 teaspoon wheat germ or ¼ teaspoon wheat-germ oil

Blend all ingredients for a few seconds in the blender for frothing up, and *voilà!* a complete health diet. (You may not care for the texture of the wheat germ in a drink. In that case you can substitute about ¼ teaspoon wheat-germ oil for the same nutrient value.)

WILDCAT'S MILK

A wonder pick-me-up for the breakfastless crowd, first thing in the morning.

1 cup yogurt
2–3 tablespoons frozen orange-juice concentrate
1 tablespoon molasses
1 ½ teaspoons brewer's yeast

Whirl all ingredients in the blender for a few seconds.

FROZEN FRUIT SMOOTHIES

Use any fruit you like for this: Raspberries, peaches, and cherries are among the favorites.

1 cup yogurt
½ 10-ounce package frozen fruit, unthawed or
thawed, with its juice

Just blend yogurt and fruit for a few seconds and drink while cold and frosty.

SODA POP

1 cup yogurt
1 cup club soda (plain or with your favorite flavoring added) or cola or ginger ale
Ice cubes

Blend yogurt and soda and pour over ice cubes for a zingy summer drink.

CLAM COCKTAIL

1 cup yogurt
½ cup clam juice or juice from canned minced clams
Chopped fresh mint (optional)

Froth up yogurt and clam juice a bit in a blender and drink soon; a bit of chopped fresh mint added would be all to the good.

CHOCOLATE DRINK

1 cup yogurt
2–3 tablespoons chocolate syrup or ca b syrup,
for the same taste and less fat and calories

Blend yogurt and syrup until foamy. If you substitute a coffee syrup, you get a coffee-flavored drink. Or use them half and half for mocha.

MAPLE COCKTAIL

1 cup yogurt
2–3 tablespoons maple syrup
1 tablespoon lemon juice
Whiskey (optional)

Whip all ingredients together in blender. Serve hot or cold. This has a fine New England taste. With the whiskey added, you have a favorite after-ski drink of Franconia, New Hampshire. Some call it Vermont Punch or Après-Ski Grog.

BEEF COCKTAIL

A hearty cold drink.

1 cup beef broth or jellied consommé
1 cup yogurt
½ teaspoon lemon juice
Parsley

Beat together the broth, yogurt, and lemon juice, blending until smooth, adding the parsley as you blend, or topping the drink with it as a garnish.

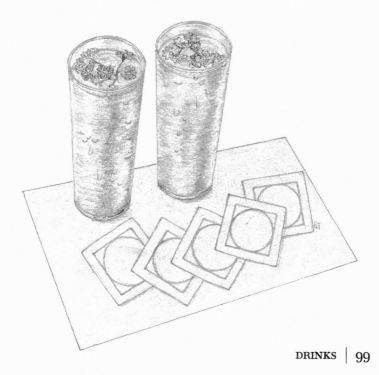

VEGETABLE COCKTAIL

Full of vitamins, this cocktail is a way to empty out your refrigerator shelves when you have just a bit of this and that left.

1 carrot, chopped
1 onion, chopped
1 lettuce leaf
1 cup celery leaves
1 cup yogurt
1 cup water

Blend all ingredients well in blender and serve cold. Work out other vegetable combinations, not overlooking the almighty tomato, either raw or in paste, sauce, or puree form.

APPLE-MINT COCKTAIL

1 cup yogurt or a combination of ½ cup yogurt
    and ½ cup buttermilk
1 cup apple juice
1 tablespoon minced fresh mint

Blend all ingredients until foamy and drink cold.

GRAPE FROST

1 cup yogurt
½ cup grape juice
1 teaspoon lemon juice

Blend all ingredients together and drink frosty cold.

ORANGE BLOSSOM

1 cup yogurt
¼ cup frozen orange-juice concentrate
3–4 tablespoons watercress

Blend all ingredients together. If you have no
blender, chop watercress and stir everything up well.
(A jigger of gin would turn this into the traditional
Orange Blossom, but this recipe will be a wholesome,
vitaminy blossom.)

The following drinks are alcoholic, but they are quite
palatable without the liquor.

ANEMIC BLOODY MARY

3 cups tomato juice

1 cup yogurt

1 teaspoon Worcestershire sauce

1 squirt Tabasco

2 jiggers vodka

Stir or blend or mix together all ingredients and serve cold. (Then don't try to stand up too soon.)

Serves 4.

TANGERINE RUM

2 cups yogurt

1 cup tangerine juice

1 cup rum

1 orange, peeled, seeded, and sliced

Blend first 3 ingredients together. The orange slices may also be added to the mixture in the blender, or they may be slipped in at serving time to float and dress the drink up. Serve hot or cold. Of course, you may transpose and use 1 cup orange juice and floating tangerine sections—or any other combination of citrus fruits; lime and grapefruit would be nice.

Serves 4.

Some people drink Scotch in milk; others don't. The former might combine Scotch and liquid yogurt. But probably the best use for yogurt in alcoholic drinks is in eggnogs and their relatives. Here are several varieties of noggy drinks, all recommended for holiday party-giving.

BRANDY EGGNOG

2 cups yogurt
4 egg yolks
1 tablespoon sugar or ¾ teaspoon honey
2 cups fruit brandy (apricot, peach, cherry, or
   blackberry)
4 egg whites
Nutmeg

Beat together 1 cup of the yogurt, the 4 egg yolks, the sugar, and the fruit brandy and chill for a few hours. Just before serving, whip together until stiff the remaining yogurt and the 4 egg whites. Fold into the first mixture. Sprinkle the top of each cupful of the nog with nutmeg before serving.

Yield: 12 cups.

COCOA NOG

2 cups crème de cacao
2 cups yogurt
Ice cubes
2 cups club soda

Shake up liqueur and yogurt with ice cubes and pour liquid into cups, discarding ice cubes. Add soda just before serving.

Yield: 12 cups.

KENTUCKY EGGNOG

2 cups yogurt
1 cup sugar or ½ cup honey or corn syrup (light
   or dark)
2 cups bourbon
4 eggs, separated
Nutmeg (optional)

Beat together yogurt, sugar, bourbon, and egg yolks. Just before serving, beat egg whites until stiff and fold into yogurt mixture. Sprinkle cupfuls of the eggnog with nutmeg if you wish.

Yield: 12 cups.

EGGNOG VERT

Follow all the directions for Brandy Eggnog (see page 103) except substitute crème de menthe for the fruit brandy. A beautiful and clean-tasting libation.

Yield: 12 cups.

GINGER SPICE

4 cups yogurt
2 cups ginger brandy
1 teaspoon sugar or ½ teaspoon honey
2 cups water
Lemon slices
Cloves
Cinnamon

Mix first 4 ingredients together until smooth. Garnish each serving with lemon slices, a few cloves, and a sprinkle of cinammon (or a stick of cinnamon if you have one). Serve either hot or cold.

Yield: 8 cups.

Chapter 11
DESSERTS

Dessert, in our culture, usually means something sweet. The dishes that follow can be distinguished from the yogurt specialties in earlier parts of the book by their decided appeal to that prominent American sweet tooth. They can be made more or less saccharine, to your taste. Since I have been persuaded of how really bad for you standard white sugar is (a whole book on this subject has been published), you will find that honey often appears where you might have expected white sugar to be listed. But if honey too is not part of your diet, you may want to substitute corn syrup, molasses, or some other sweetener. Or just leave the recipe unsweetened—you won't reduce the yogurt's value to your insides that way. (The cold desserts come first in this chapter; those that must be baked are at the end.)

YOGURT POPS

The simplest frozen yogurt dessert is Yogurt Pops, any flavor. The way to make them is to mix your flavoring—chocolate sauce, vanilla extract, honey, maple syrup, fruit syrup, citrus concentrates, or whatever—with your yogurt, then fill your ice-cube trays ⅔ full. Now get together your collection of chopsticks, Popsicle sticks, plant markers, tongue depressors, or any other bits of wood and stick 1 into the middle of the yogurt in each ice-cube cup. And freeze. Just as you would ice cubes. *Voila,* Yogurt Pops, for fun and refreshment.

COOKIE FREEZE

The next easiest frozen yogurt dessert is made by laying your favorite sweet, thin cookies on the bottom of a refrigerator tray, standing some of them up along the sides, filling the tray with yogurt, and freezing. (You may have to let this stand, after freezing, in the kitchen for a bit before you cut it up to serve for dessert.)

Serves 8–10.

MAPLE FREEZE

1 cup maple syrup
3 egg whites
1 cup thick yogurt

Cook the syrup over medium heat to the soft-ball stage (when a bit of syrup dropped into cold water forms a ball that holds its shape in the water but can be easily flattened with fingers when removed from water). Beat the egg whites until stiff, add the syrup, and beat until cool. Now combine with the yogurt, pour into a freezer tray, and freeze.

If you don't freeze it solid, you will save the yogurt bacteria from death. In that case, when it is partially frozen, remove from freezing compartment and beat, then put back into refrigerator to keep.

Serves 4–6.

All the rest of the recipes in this chapter can be prepared without killing your yogurt. Put the dish into the freezing compartment for just the shortest time or merely place it in the refrigerator.

¾ cup macaroon crumbs (made in blender)
1 tablespoon Cointreau or Cognac
3 egg whites
½ cup powdered sugar
2 cups thick yogurt

Sprinkle the macaroon crumbs with the Cointreau. Beat the egg whites until very stiff, adding sugar slowly as you beat. Now add the yogurt and ½ the crumbs to the whites. Spoon the mixture into paper cups, packing it down hard. Sprinkle the rest of the crumbs on top and cover with foil or wax paper. Store in refrigerator for a few days before eating.

Yield: 10 small cups.

3 eggs
2 egg yolks
1 tablespoon grated lemon rind
¼ cup honey
½ cup lemon juice
1 envelope unflavored gelatin
2 cups thick yogurt
1 cup strawberries

Beat eggs and extra yolks until frothy, adding lemon rind and honey slowly as you beat (or use blender). In top of double boiler combine lemon juice and gelatin and stir over hot water until gelatin is dissolved. Beat into eggs, adding yogurt, until mixture is quite stiff. Pour into a glass dish and refrigerate. Serve with strawberries on top.

Serves 6.

1 8-ounce can crushed pineapple, drained
1 cup marshmallows (small ones or quartered
large ones)
1 ½ cups thick yogurt
2 teaspoons lemon juice
Coconut shreds (optional)

Combine pineapple and marshmallows and refrigerate several hours. Just before serving, fold in yogurt and lemon juice and serve (with some coconut shreds on top if you wish).

Serves 4.

DATE-NUT MOUSSE

A rich and delicious gourmet dish.

1 envelope unflavored gelatin
1 tablespoon cold water
2 cups thick yogurt
1 tablespoon honey
½–1 cup dates, chopped
½–1 cup nuts, chopped

Prepare the gelatin by melting it in the water in the top of a double boiler over simmering water. Then stir it into the yogurt, adding the honey. Add the dates and nuts, distributing them evenly, and pour into a glass dish. Refrigerate for several hours.

Serves 4.

RASPBERRY PARFAIT

1 10-ounce package frozen raspberries (or equal volume fresh)
½ cup yogurt
1 3-ounce package cream cheese
1 tablespoon honey

Put berries (thawed, if frozen, only until you can cut them in chunks) in blender and run it at low speed for a few seconds. Then blend the remaining ingredients separately until smooth. Spoon berries and yogurt mixture alternately into parfait glasses and serve.

Serves 4.

HONEY PIE

This tastes much more fattening than it is.

- 1 cup yogurt
- 1 9-ounce package cream cheese, softened
- 1 tablespoon honey
- ½ teaspoon vanilla extract
- 1 baked pie shell

Combine the first 4 ingredients, fill the pie shell with the mixture, and refrigerate.

Serves 6–8.

CREPES

1 egg, beaten
½ cup all-purpose flour
¾ cup milk
1 tablespoon sugar
1 tablespoon grated lemon rind
1 tablespoon Cognac
Butter
Sugar (optional)
2 cups yogurt
Raspberry jam
Confectioners' sugar

To the beaten egg, alternately add the flour and milk, a little of each at a time, mixing very well. Add the sugar, lemon rind, and Cognac. Lightly grease a flat, heavy pan and heat until quite hot. Spoon in ¼ of the batter, tilting the pan to spread thinly. Turn crepe when bubbles appear on the top and cook a moment on the other side. Remove and butter. Sprinkle with sugar (if you wish), then spoon ¼ of the yogurt into the center and roll up. Keep warm while you repeat the process with the rest of the batter, making 3 more crepes. Spread the crepes with jam and top with a sprinkling of confectioners' sugar.

Yield: 4 crepes.

A very tony light dessert to serve after a robust meal.

1 bunch seedless green grapes
2 cups yogurt
Brown sugar or maple sugar (optional)
Nutmeg or cinnamon (optional)

Simply remove the stems and any sticks or leaves from grapes, stir them up in the yogurt, and chill. When you are ready to serve, sprinkle top with sugar or spice or both.

Serves 4–8.

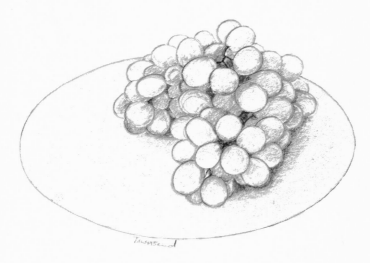

MOCHA BAVARIAN CREAM

1 envelope unflavored gelatin
½ cup cold water
2 tablespoons instant coffee
6 ounces sweet or semisweet chocolate
1 tablespoon sugar or 1 ½ teaspoons honey
1 ½ cups milk, scalded
2 egg yolks
1 cup thick yogurt

Dissolve the gelatin in cold water. Blend in the instant coffee. Mix the chocolate and sugar or honey into the milk; heat gently until chocolate melts. Cool mixture and add the coffee gelatin, egg yolks, and yogurt, blending all until smooth. Pour into a glass dish and refrigerate until set.

Serves 6–8.

RICE PUDDING

1 envelope unflavored gelatin
½ cup cold water
3 cups thick yogurt
½ cup confectioners' sugar or ¼ cup honey
½ teaspoon vanilla extract
4 cups cold cooked rice

Dissolve gelatin in cold water. Stir it into the yogurt, together with the sugar and vanilla. Then add the rice (put it through a strainer first if you want a smoother-textured pudding). Spoon pudding into a dish and refrigerate.

Serves 4–6.

1 16-ounce can fruit cocktail with its syrup
6 cups thick yogurt
1 tablespoon lemon juice
1 egg white (optional)

Blend first 3 ingredients in the blender until nearly smooth—if you want this sort of texture—pour into a dish, and refrigerate. If you want to retain the given shapes of the fruits, just stir them and their syrup into the yogurt and lemon juice with a wooden spoon and refrigerate. A third method is to combine the fruit and syrup, yogurt, and lemon juice either by blender or by hand and pour the mixture into a bowl. Put it in the freezer and freeze just until mushy, then remove it and beat it up with the egg white before refrigerating it.

Serves 6.

ORANGE SHERBET

2 cups yogurt
1 cup orange juice
1 cup corn syrup or other syrup
1 tablespoon lemon juice
3 egg whites

Beat up the first 4 ingredients. Put into ice-cube tray and into freezer until it has just begun to freeze. Remove and beat in the egg whites until the mixture is quite stiff. Then refrigerate.

Serves 4–6.

FIGS SUPREME

1 quart yogurt
1 cup dates, chopped
8–12 fresh or dried figs, sliced
1 orange or tangerine, peeled, seeded, and sliced
1 cup honey
1 cup shredded coconut

Mix together all ingredients and chill. Then figure out other combinations of fruits, nuts, and seeds.

Serves 8–12.

MARMALADE DESSERT

1 cup yogurt
1 tablespoon marmalade or preserves
1 teaspoon brown sugar

Mix all the ingredients together and refrigerate. If it isn't sweet enough as it is, sprinkle some more brown sugar on top as you eat it. Particularly good this way are ginger, peach, quince, and greengage marmalades. Calorie-ful, of course.

Serves 1.

2 cups claret wine

1 tablespoon honey

Pinch cinnamon

2 cups sweet red cherries, stems removed, pitted
or not

1 tablespoon currant jelly

1 cup yogurt

Mix wine with honey and cinnamon, pour over cherries, and cook on low heat for 10 minutes. Let cool, then remove the cherries. Cook juice some more, adding jelly, until it is a bit thickened. Let cool, stir in the yogurt, and pour over the cherries. Serve cold.

Serves 4–6.

PEACH PIE

5–6 medium-size peaches, peeled, pitted, and
    sliced
2 cups yogurt
½ cup honey
1 teaspoon cinnamon
1 teaspoon vanilla extract
¼ cup cornstarch or arrowroot
Pinch salt
1 baked pie shell

Mix all ingredients except pie shell together and pour them into shell. Refrigerate, and *voilà*, you have a peach pie. (Or leave out the pie crust, and you have peach pudding.)

Variation: Instead of peaches, use some other fruit and/or berry. A combination of boysenberry and apple would be tasty; so would blueberry and banana.

Serves 6–8.

This is a mouth-watering dessert you can make from those pumpkins you acquired at Halloween time and then left to sit on the porch or windowsill until they got frostbitten or started to cave in.

2 cups pumpkin meat
Water
2 tablespoons butter or margarine
1 cup honey
1 teaspoon cinnamon, nutmeg, or a mixture
    of both
½ cup orange juice
1 teaspoon grated orange or lemon rind
3 eggs, separated
·1 cup yogurt
2 tablespoons sherry or Cognac (optional)

Steam or simmer the pumpkin meat over or in water until tender. Strain if you like a very smooth texture; if you want it chunky, forget the strainer. Add honey, cinnamon, orange juice, orange rind, egg yolks, yogurt, and sherry if desired. Beat until smooth. Beat egg whites until stiff and fold in. Bake in a pre-heated 375° oven for 35–45 minutes or until custard is set. (If you want a pumpkin pie, just bake the pudding in a pie crust.)

Serves 6–8.

FLAN (Crème Caramel)

1 cup sugar or ½ cup honey
½ teaspoon cinnamon
1 tablespoon grated orange rind
4 cups yogurt
⅔ cup sugar
4 eggs, lightly beaten

Simmer the sugar, cinnamon, orange rind, and yogurt slowly. Meanwhile caramelize the remaining sugar by melting it over low heat in a small saucepan, moving it constantly so sugar does not burn. Pour a little caramel into each of 6 large custard dishes. Let yogurt mixture cool, then strain it into a bowl holding the eggs and blend. Remove any foam and pour into custard dishes. Place dishes in pan of cold water; water should come ⅔ of the way up their sides. Put all into a preheated 450° oven for 35 to 45 minutes or until custard is nicely browned on top.

The flavor of the yogurt makes an interesting change in this classic dish. And you can, of course, make it even more novel by varying the flavorings: In place of the orange, use lemon or lime rind, or omit the cinnamon and orange rind and add vanilla and/or almond extract, or substitute rum or Cognac for the orange and cinnamon.

Yield: 6 large custard dishes.

BAKED BANANA

1 banana
1 teaspoon honey or molasses
1 tablespoon yogurt
1 teaspoon shredded coconut

Split the banana lengthwise. Spread it with the honey, then spoon yogurt over that, and top with shredded coconut. Bake in a preheated 350° oven for 15 to 20 minutes and serve hot.

Serves 1–2.

This is a very rich cake.

1 cup yogurt
2 8-ounce packages cream cheese
3 eggs
1 cup sugar or ½ cup honey
1 tablespoon vanilla extract or 1 ½ teaspoons
    vanilla and 1 ½ teaspoons almond extract
Graham-cracker crust (made with graham crumbs,
    melted butter, brown sugar)

Topping (optional):
½ teaspoon vanilla extract
2 teaspoons honey
½ cup yogurt or sour cream

Have the first 5 ingredients at room temperature. Cream them together. Pour into crust and bake in a preheated 350° oven about 20 minutes or until a crack appears in the surface.

A topping can then be added if desired, made of the remaining ingredients mixed together. If you use the topping, turn the oven up to 400° and return the cake to the oven for 5 minutes more.

Serves 12–16.

EASY CHOCOLATE PIE

1 16½-ounce can light-chocolate ready-to-spread
    frosting
1 egg
1 3-ounce package cream cheese, softened
1 cup yogurt
¼ cup flour or arrowroot
1 unbaked pie shell (optional)

Cream together first 5 ingredients, then blend in blender until smooth. Pour into a buttered pie pan (or into pastry shell). Bake in a preheated 350° oven 45–60 minutes or until chocolate begins to pull away from sides of pan or shell. Cool before serving.

Serves 6–8.

APPLE NUT COFFEE CAKE

Coffee cake has always seemed to me more of a dessert than a breakfast, so . . .

1 cup shortening, melted
1 cup honey
2 eggs
1 teaspoon vanilla extract
2 cups flour
1 teaspoon baking powder
1 teaspoon baking soda
¼ teaspoon salt
1 cup yogurt
2 cups small apple chunks

Topping:
½ cup chopped nuts
½ cup brown sugar
1 teaspoon cinnamon
2 tablespoons melted butter or margarine

Mix together the first 4 ingredients. Sift together the next 4 ingredients. Alternatingly add some of the flour mixture, then some of the yogurt, to the egg mixture until all are combined. Fold in the apples and spread batter in a greased baking pan. Now make the topping by combining the remaining ingredients. Spread it over the cake either before or after you bake it for 35–45 minutes in a preheated 350° oven.

Serves 8–12.

JADIS'S GOOD BROWN CAKE

¼ cup margarine
1 cup brown sugar
2 eggs, lightly beaten
1¾ cups bran flour
Pinch salt
½ teaspoon baking powder
½ cup liquid yogurt
1 teaspoon mixed spices (cinnamon, nutmeg,
    allspice, or whatever you like)
¾ cup raisins

Cream margarine and brown sugar together; beat in eggs slowly. Sift flour, salt, and baking powder together and stir in. Add yogurt, spices, and raisins, stirring so that raisins are distributed evenly through batter. Turn into a greased cake pan and bake in a preheated 350° oven for about 1 hour and 10 minutes. Cool in pan for 5 minutes, then remove from pan and finish cooling on rack.

Serves 6–8.

1 cup yogurt (a "sour milk")
1 cup butter or margarine
2 eggs, separated
¾ cup molasses
2 cups flour
1 teaspoon baking soda
½ teaspoon salt
Brown sugar or a mixture of ½ brown sugar and
    ½ white sugar (optional)

Cream the yogurt, shortening, egg yolks, and molasses together. Then sift flour, baking soda, and salt together and add slowly to egg mixture, stirring until well blended. Beat the egg whites until stiff but not dry and fold them lightly into the batter. If you want a nice crispy crust on top, sprinkle the top of the batter with the sugar before baking. Bake in greased cake pan in a preheated 375° oven for about 30 minutes.

Into this cake you may be able to sneak whole-grain flour rather than the usual old white. The color will not give you away, and the molasses-yogurt taste will overpower the "wheaty" taste that keeps so many cake-eaters off cake made with nutritious flour.

Serves 6–8.

MOTHER PARKER'S SPICE CAKE

1 cup sugar

½ cup shortening (Mother Parker used lard)

1 teaspoon cloves

1 teaspoon cinnamon

1 teaspoon nutmeg

2 cups flour

1 egg, well beaten

3 tablespoons molasses

1 cup yogurt (she used sour milk, but yogurt works fine)

1 teaspoon baking soda dissolved in 1 tablespoon milk (or in the yogurt)

Mix together first 6 ingredients and set aside 1 cup for the frosting. To the remainder add the rest of the ingredients and beat well. Spread batter into greased cake pan. Cover top with reserved frosting. Bake for 45 minutes in a preheated 350° oven.

Serves 6–8.

Chapter 12

INSTEAD OF'S
AND
WHY NOT'S

Instead of butter or sour cream, why not top a beautiful baked potato with a nice fat dollop of creamy yogurt and then sprinkle some chopped chives over it?

Why not substitute liquid yogurt for the cream or milk in your soufflés or omelettes? (The other day I made an elegant soufflé with sharp Cheddar cheese and yogurt—delicious!)

Instead of adding milk and flour to your pan drippings for a yummy gravy to go with your bird or roast, why not add yogurt and arrowroot and have an equally yummy (and less fattening) gravy?

Instead of milk or cream in fondues . . . ?

Why not top your spaghetti with a garlic, yogurt, and butter sauce? (Some Armenians I know swear by it.)

Instead of milk or cream on your favorite breakfast cereal, try a little yogurt—its taste combines well with most whole grains.

Why not moisten your poultry stuffing with yogurt instead of milk or egg? Its flavor, together with the sage that I hope you put into the dressing, improves that sometimes-too-bland stuffing.

Instead of heavy or whipped cream on top of gelatin desserts?

Why not spoon some yogurt in place of clotted cream over ripe, fresh strawberries?

Instead of whipped cream or vanilla ice cream on your apple pie, how about a gob of thick, creamy yogurt? With a piece of cheese on the side, you'll *still* have a dessert as American as . . .

And instead of buying it at the grocery store and paying a highly inflated price, why not make your own yogurt? One little packet of yogurt culture can start a yogurt supply that will last you for the rest of your life if you just save at least ½ cup from each batch before you start the new one (see pages 6–10 for directions).

INDEX

Pudding
  Fancy Corn, 69
  Pumpkin, 123
  Rice, 117
Pumpkin
  Pudding, 123
  seeds, dip with, 50
Pumpkin Pudding, 123

Quiche, Spinach, 76

Radishes and endive, yo-
    gurt with, 56
Raisin
  Luncheon Bread, 39
  Salad, Carrot-, 80
Raisin Luncheon Bread,
    39
Raspberry(-ies)
  Parfait, 112
  salad dressing with, 61
  yogurt with, 54
Raspberry Parfait, 112
Red Flannel Hash, 68
Red Wine, Cherries in, 121
Rhubarb, yogurt with, 54
Rice
  Bouffant, Brown, 73
  Pudding, 117
  yogurt with, 56
Rice Pudding, 117
Rolls, Speedy, 36
Rosell   Bacteriological
    Dairy Institute, 3

Salad(s)
  Avocado   and   Bean
    Sprouts, 72

Salad(s) (cont.)
  Carrot-Raisin, 80
  dressings, 58–63
    for fruit, 61
    for green, 59–60
  fruit,   yogurt   dressing
    for, 61
  green, yogurt dressing
    for, 59–60
  Sprout, 79
  Turkey, 89
  Sandwich fillings, yogurt
    in, 59
  See also Dip(s)
Sardines,   yogurt   with,
    56
Sauce(s)
  for meat or fish, 62–63
  Oyster, Chicken in, 82
  for spaghetti, 132
  for vegetables, 58–60
  yogurt, 133
Savory Lamb, 93
Scallions, salad dressing
    with, 60
Schav (Sorrel Soup), 16
Seafood Curry, 83
Seeds
  dip with, 50
  sauce with, 62
Sherbet, Orange, 119
Shrimp Bisque, 21
Soda Pop, 97
Sorrel Soup (Schav), 16
Soufflé, made with yogurt,
    132
Soup, 14–30
  Apple, 29
  Avocado, 22
  Beet, 15